A New Man

A Memoir by
Charlie Kiss

Copyright © 2017 Charlie Kiss

The moral right of the author has been asserted.

This book is a work of non-fiction based on the life experiences and recollections of the author. In some cases, names of people and descriptions have been changed solely to protect the privacy of others.

The views and opinions expressed in the book are the author's.

Apart from any fair dealing for the purposes of research or private study, or criticism or review, as permitted under the Copyright, Designs and Patents Act 1988, this publication may only be reproduced, stored or transmitted, in any form or by any means, with the prior permission in writing of the publishers, or in the case of reprographic reproduction in accordance with the terms of licences issued by the Copyright Licensing Agency. Enquiries concerning reproduction outside those terms should be sent to the publishers.

Matador
9 Priory Business Park,
Wistow Road, Kibworth Beauchamp,
Leicestershire. LE8 0RX
Tel: 0116 279 2299
Email: books@troubador.co.uk
Web: www.troubador.co.uk/matador
Twitter: @matadorbooks

ISBN 978 1788036 047
British Library Cataloguing in Publication Data.
A catalogue record for this book is available from the British Library.

Printed and bound by CPI Group (UK) Ltd, Croydon, CR0 4YY

Matador is an imprint of Troubador Publishing Ltd

Dedicated to trans men everywhere
and to anyone who has been incarcerated
for mental health problems.

Contents

	Introduction	1
1	Epiphany	3
2	Colombia to London	5
3	Being David	12
4	To Yorkshire	23
5	The Life Saver: Punk	31
6	Joining the Lesbian Community	40
7	Greenham Common Women's Peace Camp	52
8	Imprisonment	62
9	Escaping to Holloway Prison	75
10	The Swiss Dream	89
11	Leaving Greenham	98
12	Breakdown	105
13	Lipstick Lesbian	113
14	Mania	121
15	Mental Hospital	130
16	B&B Accommodation & Council Flat	134
17	Unable to Marry	144
18	Relapse	153
19	Split Identities	162
20	Becoming a 'New Man'	171
21	Living as a Man	185
22	Surgery in Belgium	196
	Epilogue	205
	Note on Terminology	208
	Acknowledgements	209

Introduction

Until my early thirties, I lived my life as a lesbian, much of it in a separatist lifestyle. Lesbianism, and its implied strength and independence from men, was my identity first and foremost. I knew one thing for certain: I was attracted to women. I felt proud to be a lesbian, much more so than being a woman, and I was determined to avoid subservience to men. Most lesbian separatists, including me, believed that men were the main cause of so many women's problems.

Men's domination of the world order made me angry. I saw my mother, a strong and talented woman, treated as a second-class citizen; there were fewer opportunities and choices open to women, to me, consequently I despised sexism and the power men had.

Then one day I woke up and had an epiphany. Previous feelings about being male had been repressed but not this time. This morning, I couldn't deny it. It was crystal clear: I wanted, and needed, to transition to male.

At the time, nearly all my friends were lesbians and I thought it was highly unlikely that I would get a positive reaction or encouragement from any of them about being transsexual.

But I harboured a greater fear still. In my twenties, I had suffered destructive episodes of severe mental illness and had an identity crisis. I was not prepared to risk returning to that state no matter the personal discomfort and continuing sexual problems I had.

So, I concluded that the seemingly obvious resolution to problems in my relationships and the achievement of my childhood dream to be male had to stay unachievable. I told myself I would just have to accept myself as I was and make the best of things.

People often say you're influenced by your upbringing but there is still little consensus about how much is shaped by the environment or

A New Man

genetics, nature or by nurture. I don't know why some people feel that they have an inherent trait of being a different gender to the one presumed at birth based on external physical characteristics, but for me it was simply the conflict between how I expected my body to be and the reality of having a female body. It was fundamentally a physical and sexual issue and this had always been my reality.

I know without question, that since changing to male emotionally and biologically through the injection of male hormones, physically through surgery and of course socially has meant that I feel far more comfortable and happier in myself. This is my story of the long journey of how I got there.

1

Epiphany

I sat bolt upright in bed. Saturday morning sunlight crept in around the drawn curtains. I was lost in thought. An idea had been building in my mind, and as I lay in bed it crystallized until I blurted out loud, 'That's it, I must be transsexual!'

The idea felt blindingly obvious. I felt certain and exhilarated. I was in my early 30s, in my treasured council flat in Kilburn and in an 'on/off' relationship. Carol lay in bed beside me, trying to pull the duvet back down. She said, 'Don't be ridiculous! Of course, you're not!' She rolled over on her side and tried to go back to sleep.

The night before, we'd had sex with most of our clothes on. I much preferred it that way, as it enabled me to deny my female body. I had turned my head and seen her bright purple varnished nails grasping my shoulders; it was so erotic, I was obviously with a heterosexual woman, at least in my fantasy. Carol had short blonde hair and dressed in a conventionally feminine way with delicate scarves, broches and flowing skirts but like most of my previous partners, considered herself a lesbian.

It dawned on me that I had never allowed myself to think properly about how I felt about the uncomfortable truth that I didn't have what I yearned for – a man's body. I couldn't come without fantasising about having male genitals and I simply felt disconnected from the body I had been dealt. I tried other fantasies of being a woman desperately and I tried to be in the present but I always reverted to being male, every single time.

I found it very difficult to enjoy being touched, which meant sex was often one-sided, with me giving pleasure. With Carol, I fantasised that I was the eager young man seducing an older yet inexperienced woman.

A New Man

I had been confused on hearing that many butch, masculine-appearing lesbians were comfortable having a female body, didn't behave butch in bed and even liked to be penetrated. Conversely with me, although I didn't appear that butch, my body was clearly guarded, with several 'out of bounds' signs.

Sometimes lovers told me that I had nice breasts, which I could just about cope with but if anyone touched them I reacted badly. Once I forcefully pushed my partner away in anger and another time it happened, I threw a plate against the wall. I usually wore T-shirts in bed to cover them up or I'd lie on my front, enabling me to feel I was a man.

My desire to have male genitalia overwhelmed me to the point that I even watched gay men's porn so that I could focus on masculine sexuality rather than being forced to remember that I had a female body. But I never felt attracted to men.

On this morning, I tried to ignore Carol's dismissal. Absorbed in thoughts that my body should have been male, that in fact I was male, I got out of bed, took off my t-shirt and underwear and walked over to the full-length mirror and looked at myself completely naked.

In a new light, I saw more clearly than usual. I saw a woman's body with my male head on it, objectively a reasonable female body but looking completely incongruous with my head. I flexed my biceps, which made me feel slightly better. I didn't have a bad set of muscles and at least I had been blessed with broad shoulders.

Thoughts crowded into my head. How could I desire a male body? I'm a feminist. Changing into a man is utterly unacceptable. I have a healthy body, why seek medical intervention to change it? Was I prepared to be seen as a man in everyday life? It just felt too much to even contemplate.

Indeed, it was too much. I decided I would just cope the best I could. I bottled up my feelings and suppressed my yearning to be male. I didn't mention the subject again to Carol.

2

Colombia to London

Knowing where you come from is essential for a sense of identity. Knowing your gender is even more critical. I was born in London and given a girl's name easily shortened to Charlie. My original birth certificate identified me as female, a fact that I spent half my life coming to terms with as an error, but at least I knew who my parents were and I knew I was from London.

My mother, Marta Lombard, wasn't sure where she was from and didn't find out who her parents were until she was an adult. She was despatched from Colombia on her own aged only six to a convent in Haywards Heath in Sussex. Then later, just before her confirmation, she was installed in an Anglo-Colombian family in Finchley, North London. The only person who showed any interest in her was an uncle from Colombia, called Jaime Jaramillo Arango. Jaime would visit Marta periodically.

As soon as Marta was old enough, she left the home in Finchley where she had been very unhappy and moved in with other students when she started studying fine art at the Central School of Art and Design in London. It was then that she confronted Jaime, who had been visiting her all these years and paying for her upbringing, and he admitted that he was in fact her father. Jaime had had an affair with Marta's mother and Marta consequently had to be hidden. Her mother, Ana Rosa, wanted as little as possible to do with Marta. Jaime tried to do the best for her but as a travelling diplomat he couldn't look after her properly so he put her in the convent.

At college, Marta met my dad, Geoffrey Kiss, who was studying graphic design. 'Kiss' is a common Hungarian name: Emeric Kiss, Dad's Great Granddad, had emigrated from Hungary to London around 1880.

A New Man

My dad had a more stable background than Marta, although his parents divorced when he was thirteen. He was born in Isleworth and brought up in a small bungalow in Feltham.

Feltham in those days was a peaceful area of London, as the London Airport in Heathrow close by had not yet been developed.

As he got older, he became a socialist; his parents were working class, non-religious and had always voted Labour. Dad also became interested in humanism and vegetarianism in his twenties. My mother had been raised a Catholic, but she was a questioning Catholic. She was also interested in left-wing ideas, seeing community and relationships as far more important than material wealth.

In 1959, after Dad had completed his national service in Germany, they married in the Catholic Church of St Thomas More in Hampstead. Jaime, was unwell and far away in Colombia, so he and his wife didn't attend Marta's wedding. Marta's mother, Ana Rosa, continued to refuse to acknowledge Marta was her daughter so she was also not going to attend.

As a teenager, Marta had often run away distraught and unhappy to a kind priest, Father Lawler, who was understanding. It was fitting then that at the wedding, he stood in her father's place.

Two years after the wedding Marta and Geoffrey had their first child. My sister Justina was born in January 1961. Jaime sent a cheque to Marta every month and this helped her study for a teaching qualification at Goldsmith's and pay for an au pair for Justina.

Relations, between Marta and Jaime were strained, as unsurprisingly Marta longed to have loving parents around her when she was growing up, however, Jaime did at least help her financially. Having been a surgeon then the Colombian Ambassador to the UK, he was reasonably wealthy, though Marta craved and valued emotional security much more. Marta's insecure upbringing influenced the way I was raised; she instilled in me the need to be independent and self-reliant from an early age.

Marta, Dad and Justina were planning to visit Colombia and they were even considering moving there which Jaime was keen for them to do. He felt that Marta, being a foreigner would always be at a disadvantage in the UK. But Jaime suddenly died of a heart attack in 1962, just a few months before they were due to go. His untimely death ruled out any potential move to Colombia, especially as Marta found it impossible to legally prove that she was his daughter and obtain all that was owed to her. It could be said that not moving to Colombia turned out to be fortuitous, as the country plunged deeper into a long civil war over the huge inequalities in wealth and land control and many of Marta's relatives emigrated. My life would have been very different had I been born and raised in Colombia.

Instead I was born in London. I was born at St Mary's Hospital, Paddington, on July 21st, 1965 at 1.20am, just missing Colombian Independence Day on July 20th which disappointed Marta. I can say exactly where and when I was born and who my parents were. I felt for Marta, as apart from her name, she couldn't rely on her official documentation for the truth. Her baptism document and her passport were falsified, so where her father's name should have been written, the fictitious name of Maurice Lombard was inserted instead, chosen after the famous actress, Carole Lombard.

We were living in a rented flat in Kilburn when Dad obtained a full-time job teaching at an art college in Worthing. Dad later became interested in one of the students at the college. The marriage faltered and they separated. It was not at all amicable and having been raised a Catholic, Marta found it particularly difficult.

Dad moved permanently to Brighton when I was two years old. From then on, I saw much less of him and only at occasional weekends. I was too young to understand what had happened but I was distressed having to say goodbye at railway stations on Sundays and felt sad because everyone around me was too.

Two years later, Marta met someone new named Colin, at a party. They became involved and then he moved into the Kilburn flat with the three of us. Colin was very different from Dad, not a vegetarian and nowhere near as fastidious. He was hippy-like and he introduced us to hitching; we would even hitch as a family which meant I considered

A New Man

it normal. So much so that once when I was five years old, on a family day out at the seaside, I started hitching on my own. Marta turned around and started to panic because she couldn't see me. I had gone off on my own. I had climbed over the dunes and gone to stand by the side of the road with my thumb sticking out. I wanted to go back to London to the sweet shop. She saw me and grabbed me off the road, reassuring me that we'd get some sweets later.

I was due to start primary school in Kilburn when Colin and Marta decided to leave London and move to the countryside and so one day everything was loaded into a huge lorry and we drove off to the west country.

To choose where to go to they had blindly stuck a pin on a map of the South West and we headed towards that point without knowing where we would stay that night. We slept in tents on a farm for the first few weeks and then found a house to rent in Devon called 'Little Fair Oak'. This was incredibly idyllic; the house had a part-thatched roof and came with a small field.

The plan was to have a smallholding in the countryside, a little farm. We bought a cow, two goats, two pigs, rabbits, chickens and cats and a dog. We had no comforts like carpets or an oven, a television or even a telephone.

From the crowded, busy and lively Kilburn area in London with trains running behind us all hours, and with people from the pub, 'the Rifle Volunteer', making a racket going home we had moved to the complete opposite. We were now surrounded by the noises of nature and occasional farm machinery instead of trains, cars, buses, lorries and noisy drunk revellers.

Marta was thrilled to have moved to the quiet and peaceful countryside. Sometimes we'd walk late at night down country lanes in the total darkness save a torch, singing songs and I'd look up in the sky at the thousands of stars. Marta, Justina and me even lay down in the middle of the road once, tired from carrying a heavy sewing machine Marta had found at a bargain shop; it was so quiet.

I learnt to cycle not long after moving as I could no longer walk to the nearest sweet shop. We were so isolated that mobile grocery shops and library vans came to our doorstep regularly. The lanes were so narrow they could only take a single vehicle at a time. It could not have been more different from London.

I feel an attachment to London, where I started out in life. I relish the lively atmosphere where everything you need is practically on your doorstep and I appreciate the huge variety in shops and cafes from the many different people who live there. Difference is much more accepted in London. It's a place where you can be yourself. The change in our lives was huge and I wished, especially when I became a teenager, that we had stayed in London.

I had to say goodbye to my first friends in diverse Kilburn. In Devon, there were only white faces. I had had a friend called Po who had an Indian background. Po had a very long plait and Marta and Colin were surprised to discover Po was a boy. I wasn't particularly bothered about gender at this age, Po was simply my friend. As a five-year-old I was given a lot of freedom and there was very little that was gender related which was forced on me. My mum would sometimes make me wear skirts and give me girlish hairstyles but that was about the extent of me being put in a female role. I wasn't pushed, prevented, encouraged or discouraged from so-called boy's toys or girl's toys, I was simply given the option to choose. I mostly wanted the toys that boys wanted however, and was especially fond of my many cars.

At the primary school in Devon, Justina and I, were singled out as strange. Not long after we had started at the new school, an older girl called us gypsies and said that we were dirty; others joined in. We had lived in tents, that was true, and we had very slightly darker skin, and looked Mediterranean or Latino, though this was much more obvious with Justina. We complained to Marta about this and she just replied, 'Well you are a bit dirty!' pointing to the mud on my knee. This was typical of her tough approach. At least at school, I had an older sister who I could call on when needed, but it wasn't to last.

Marta, it turned out, had not told Dad our new address in Devon. He managed to track us down though and they wrote hurtful letters

A New Man

to each other and divorce proceedings started through solicitors. I dreamt that I saw Dad in the distance on a high street when we were out shopping. I called out to him, 'Dad! Dad!' but he couldn't hear me and then I saw him disappear into the crowd. I was sad losing him and now we lived in Devon, it was impossible to see him much.

When visiting him in Brighton, he regularly took us to Preston Park, which he lived opposite, and we would run around playing and hiding behind the unusual clock tower there. I missed his enthusiasm for me and my sister. I missed being lifted onto his shoulders and holding his bald head. Dad always gave me crushing hugs, practically squeezing the breath out of me, when we met up. I could tell he cared. Once when staying with him in his flat in Brighton, I wrote a message on a big bit of wood. I went up to him and placed it in his hands. He was overwhelmed. I'd written, 'Dear Daddy please don't forget me.'

The judge granted Marta custody of both of us. Marta and Colin got married. It was after the divorce and getting a step-dad that I started calling my mum, Marta. As I didn't want to call Colin 'Dad', it seemed less awkward to call them both by their first names. I'm not sure if it was suggested but I started doing it and, later, friends would comment that it was strange.

After the divorce, as I was still young I generally just bumbled along but Justina found it much more difficult; she missed Dad immensely and there were fierce disagreements between her and Colin. She bitterly resented Colin assuming Dad's role. Colin seemed carefree and relaxed but he was in many respects mean spirited and would often be unpleasant. He dampened my enthusiasm. Colin was busy growing vegetables. I had become excited about the idea of growing things and I wanted to join in too. Colin reluctantly agreed and, excited - I dashed out with my spade but then Colin showed me where my allotted patch was. He had given me the worst area possible, a tiny square right next to the cottage wall which was continually covered in chimney soot, I attempted to make it work but soon gave up.

Colin was quite a tough character, who worked hard and expected others too as well. He looked down on weakness and didn't seem to make sufficient allowances for children. Once he made Justina and a visiting friend of hers, help him hold the piglets whilst he castrated them without anaesthetic. He slapped Justina hard across the face once, when she answered him back. I was suspicious of him but the relationship between him and Justina was much worse as he insisted he was now 'Dad' and Justina understandably, rejected this.

Marta began to think Justina might be better off living with Dad and asked her if she'd prefer to live in Brighton with him. Justina said yes. So, now ten years old, Justina left us in the countryside and moved to Brighton to live with Dad and Jan, his new partner. Jan made it clear to Justina that she was not a substitute mother which Justina was reassured to hear.

It was a monumental decision leaving us and one which, years later, Marta said she regretted. However, Justina was relieved to be away from Colin.

I was left behind, that's what it felt like. I was missing out. I asked to go to Brighton too. I wasn't taken seriously; instead I was given a pen and paper and shown by Marta and Colin how to write my new last name: 'Reynolds'. I felt awkward and compromised.

Later that evening, Justina took me to one side in our bedroom and said to me defiantly, 'You must promise me, when you're older, to ask for 'Kiss', your real name, back'.

'Yes, I will,' I agreed solemnly.

From then on, I was effectively brought up as an only child.

3

Being David

At Little Fair Oak, from about the age of about six, I had to make cups of tea, clean and help with cooking and many of the other chores, just as Marta had to when she was little. Lighting the gas on the cooker was a bit daunting and I would gingerly put the match against the gas ring until the flames suddenly appeared with a loud noise, always startling me.

Although I was now on my own and therefore couldn't share chores or experiences with my sister anymore, there were upsides of being left behind. There were fewer fights between us obviously, as I hardly saw Justina, and I also got more attention.

Before long, we were on the move again though. The money coming in wasn't enough to enable us to stay at Little Fair Oak. It was decided that Colin should go agricultural college to learn more about farming. The plan was that he would share the knowledge with Marta though this didn't happen. To be close enough to the college we moved to a picturesque little village called Otterton, still within Devon. Marta worked as an auxiliary nurse at odd times to pay for our upkeep whilst Colin was in college. I had many different babysitters, usually students from the college, who would bathe me and put to me to bed.

I was miserable in my new school; there were only two other girls in my class and they were best friends, this made me the odd one out and I was bullied by the boys in the class. I didn't mind where I fitted in, with boys or girls, I just wanted to fit in. Being a relative newcomer added to my sense of being ostracised. Cycling along the road once, I saw a fist come at me from the corner of my eye on my left side, and I was thumped hard. The force of the blow knocked me off my bike. One of the boys from school had been standing on the door step which led directly onto the road and had decided to hit me. Marta was furious and went to see his mother who challenged him but of course he denied it. Another time a gang of boys threw stones at me. Colin tried to run after them but couldn't catch them. I was disappointed that Colin couldn't do anything to stop them. He seemed useless to me.

Happily, we didn't stay for too long in Otterton as the agricultural course was only for a year. We moved on to a much smaller village called Bathealton over the border in Somerset and I was able to leave the bullying behind.

Bathealton comprised just a few houses and two farms, it had no café or pub. All it had was a tiny shop, a church and a huge manor nearby, set apart from the houses. Colin had got a job as a herdsman on a large dairy farm near Bathealton and Marta later got a job later teaching art at the local secondary school.

I liked Somerset; we had friendly neighbours and the countryside was beautiful with rolling hills, woods and lush green fields. We lived in a semi-detached cottage right next to a brook. In a field, next to us there were five magnificent tall Lombard trees that would sway in the wind. We had a huge garden and I became firm friends with the boy living next door called Celyn.

Celyn was just a year younger than me and we got on very well with each other, playing together constantly. There was only one other child in the village but his mum wouldn't let him out to play which we thought was a shame but also really wimpish.

I fitted in at the new school and found my place. I was accepted by the boys at this school and treated as if I was one of them. At every opportunity, I'd be out playing football with them. We called each other car nicknames based on our last names. So, I was 'Renault 5TL' for my recently changed last name 'Reynolds.'

Marta passed her driving test and Celyn's mum, Jess, got on very well with mine so every Saturday morning the four of us would drive off in the Morris Minor van we had to the nearby town, Wellington. Celyn and me would sit on the wheel covers in the back imagining we were soldiers, holding our machine guns in the back of an army truck.

We went to the sports centre to the Saturday morning sports special.

A New Man

This was my idea of heaven, playing badminton or football or going on the trampoline whilst Jess and my mum bought bargains in the town's second-hand shops.

Marta made jams and wines and even set up beehives for the honey. Everyone had to help with the picking of fruits for the jam or dandelion tops or elderberries and the like for the wine. When friends of Marta or Colin's visited, we'd pick from the hedgerows often singing as we did it with the suns' heat belting down on us. Afterwards, when we got home, it would be my responsibility to make all the children orange squash and help with the dinner.

One of my tasks was taking the dog for long walks, lasting an hour or more going right up in to hills. I would always run past a notorious well said to have formerly belonged to a witch, with my adrenaline high; but walking the dog could be boring and lonely and I much preferred spending time with Celyn.

My Sundays were often the best days. I could play to my heart's content. Celyn and I would often enjoy scrambling. We'd head off on our bikes to the fields over the wooden bridge over the brook. I'd rev up my handle bar grips, as if my bike was a scrambling motorbike, and then we'd both set off scrambling, making engine noises. 'Eeerrm, eeerm,' and sliding around over the bumps in the lumpy molehill-ridden field laughing when we skidded, nearly falling off. But in the middle of the day I always had to return back to the house to lay the table for dinner. I had to wait for everyone to finish eating; with Marta, a very slow eater, I had to be patient, waiting to wash up before being able to go out and play again.

One Sunday afternoon Celyn and me decided to come out in our commando gear. Carrying our machine guns, we went into the swampy area by the trees which had become full of stinging nettles that were much taller than us. We imagined we were Royal Marine commandos in the jungle and using the butts of the guns we bashed the huge nettles down, creating a winding path until we reached the vantage point of a massive upturned tree root, then we poked our machine guns through the holes in the bottom of the tree root looking out to see if there were enemies close. The countryside was perfect for our imaginations and we often stayed out long after it got dark.

I imagined I was a real soldier. It didn't occur to me that in the future I couldn't become a royal marine or be in the parachute regiment because I was a girl. Being a girl at this age wasn't very restrictive for me. I was given a lot of freedom to do what I wanted. I was often a cowboy, an Indian or a paratrooper too. I loved dressing up and playing different roles. I was never stopped from doing something because it wasn't 'ladylike.' As I said, I was also allowed any toy I wanted which mostly was action man stuff, cars and guns. I thought that as Celyn liked making things with balsa wood, I should too but I much preferred outdoor action to crafts and I wasn't too keen on toy construction sets either which had been a surprise present from my dad.

The differences between the genders began to stand out more around the age of eight and I felt more inclined to the male side. I asked people to call me David. I wrote 'David's Room' in big black letters on a piece of card and stuck it to the outside of my bedroom door as a statement to the world. I decided I didn't want anyone to say I was a girl again and I liked my new name a lot. Dad saw the sign when he drove down to collect me once. He was concerned and discussed this with Colin and Marta. Colin apparently said it was natural and just a phase I was going through, something I am grateful for.

We had by now got a black and white telly and there was a series of James Cagney and Fred Astaire films being shown on Sunday afternoons. Marta loved these and we watched many of them together snuggled under the blankets and eating snacks. Colin was out of sight, working over the hill on the farm, not bothering us so we could relax. I imagined myself as the handsome man with the gorgeous women in these films. I felt that the world was full of possibilities; I dreamt that one day I would be romantically involved with a woman.

I started to watch a lot of sport on telly, especially Grandstand on Saturdays and I became obsessed with football. Everyone at school then supported either Leeds United FC or Liverpool FC. I chose Liverpool. I wanted to play football at home, but Celyn suffered from

A New Man

asthma, so disappointingly I had no one to play with. I put a poster up in my bedroom of Johan Cruyff who was the greatest footballer in the world at the time and wished I could be a great footballer too. Women's football was practically unheard of in 1974, which wasn't long after the FA ban on women and girls playing was lifted in 1971. Naturally then, all my footballing heroes were men, but at this age, I didn't see myself as different from the boys.

Playing football constantly in the breaks at school got me noticed by the games teacher and one day he told me to look at the selection posted up on the notice board. I had been picked to play for the primary school football team. I was extremely excited and daunted to have been selected. I had a slight problem, though as I didn't own football boots. I didn't think to ask for a pair from Marta, I just borrowed a friends' pair but these turned out to be far too small.

My very first appearance on a proper football pitch was a disaster as the boots were so painful. I was given another chance, and I wore normal trainers and could therefore play properly but my football career was to be abruptly stopped because in those days' girls were forbidden to play football past primary school.

For my ninth birthday, I had a party in the garden in the scorching hot weather, which was a lot of fun. We played some games and had a fancy-dress competition. Marta put a lot of effort into the party but I saw a momentary look of envy in her eyes when she presented me with a birthday cake. I was confused by this but I later found out she'd never been given a birthday cake and once she recounted to me that, instead of a present, her mother in Colombia had once given her coal for being 'evil', so it was understandable that her feelings sometimes showed.

Other times, she'd be incredibly warm, supportive and hug me. Marta was strong, independent and a forceful character. I learnt to understand the reason for her strange behaviour was being raised without parental love and care. Her punishments were odd, she'd make me have a bath and scrub me hard until I was, in her eyes 'clean and pure' and then she would send me to bed, closing the curtains shut in the middle of the day telling me to be completely quiet. Marta had grown up with-

Being David

out love yet she loved me. When I became an adult, she would sometimes remind me that she didn't have a mum or a dad when little. Once we watched a film called 'The Bear', which was about a little bear that survived on its own without its mum. She cried non-stop until the end.

Now I had reached the age of nine, Marta decided an important milestone had been reached as it was time for me to be more responsible. She made a firm declaration, 'You're old enough now, you don't need to have Santa anymore.' I was disappointed but Marta was determined, I could see this wasn't something I could challenge. I was already envious of Celyn's huge Santa pillow sack, as I only had a stretchy sock usually stuffed full of satsumas together with some chocolate but now I wasn't even going to have that. It wasn't fair but as Colin continually reminded me, 'Life isn't fair.'

Marta pulled out the twin tub washing machine from under the kitchen counter and proceeded to demonstrate how to use it. 'You've got to make sure the clothes are evenly distributed around the drum,' she said, 'This is how much washing powder you need, it's not difficult.' I had hung clothes on the line before but now I was nine I had to wash my own clothes as well. I didn't particularly mind. I felt I was almost a 'grown up,' and fairly independent and this was something to be proud of.

My teddy that I'd named Coffee was given away to the jumble sale too. I was sad about that, not that I looked after him that well. I used to punch him regularly in fact when I was frustrated about things but he'd been around for a while and I was still fond of him. I didn't want to make a fuss and I certainly didn't want to appear like a baby, which would have had no effect anyway, so I said nothing.

Colin worked over the hill on the farm and consequently I didn't see him that much, nor did I have much desire to. Marta and Colin argued a lot and there were often scenes. One Christmas morning after returning from milking the cows, Colin decided to go for a walk as the dinner wasn't quite ready. Whilst walking, he was stung by a wasp on his mouth and his lip swelled up. When Marta saw him, she was taken aback at how bad he looked and said tactlessly that he looked like a monster.

A New Man

Colin was furious at this but he didn't say anything. Instead he just lifted the wooden dining table right up into the air. The table had been laid beautifully, with place mats, crackers, china candle stick holders, plates, dishes, bowls with food and wine glasses ready for the big meal. Everything came crashing down, much of the crockery and glasses broke and the food splattered on the floor in a big mess. Christmas was often full of tension and it was at times like these, when I wished I was with Dad and Justina in Brighton.

I tried to get on with Colin but it wasn't easy. He was a disciplinarian and task-master in every area of life, work and pleasure. Sometimes the three of us went on arduous long walks of about eight to ten miles, across moors which I hated as Colin would stride ahead with his binoculars looking at birds. Marta would be behind following with difficulty and then there'd be me right at the back tired and struggling to keep up.

Breaks in Brighton staying with my Dad and his partner were luxurious in comparison. They lived in a comfortable house in the middle of the city with the shops just a few minutes away.

At holiday times, to get to Brighton I would be taken to the train station at Taunton, bought comics and sweets and then put on a train. I was supposed to be met at Paddington station. On one such occasion, I carried my little black suitcase off the train and started walking along the platform expecting to meet Dad, when I heard a loud voice over the tannoy telling me to make my way to the railway office on platform one.

I was startled and thought people around me could tell that it was me that was being referred to. I steeled myself and thought I must do as I'd been instructed. I had to find this office on platform one. So, I made my way anxiously and quickly to platform one, wondering where Dad was, and I started walking along it, looking for the office. There were a lot of offices. I couldn't work out which one I was supposed to go to. I began to panic wondering what I should next. I was unsure about what to do. I walked back to the main concourse and in despair and leant up against a pillar and cried. I was there for what seemed like ages, but then suddenly Dad's head appeared around the pillar. There he was. Everything was okay again. He explained that as he knew he was going to be late he thought it was best to call the station. I pleaded with him never to do that again. Although I was proud of not needing adults for every little thing, and was quite tough compared to most young girls, I also felt let down at times like this. In the Seventies, children were given much more freedom, so it wasn't considered outrageous that I'd be travelling on my own at the age of nine, but these experiences of being met late, which happened quite a lot, made me feel insecure. My mum also had a habit of disappearing too. We'd be walking down the road and she'd suddenly nip into a shop. I was often left wandering around trying to work out where she'd gone and I usually had to wait by the car as it was drummed into me that would be the best place to meet up again.

Sometimes my sister would be in Brighton when I stayed there so I'd spend time with her and other times, we'd swap and she would be in Somerset with mum and Colin, sometimes with me there and sometimes not. Not living together and not growing up together prevented us becoming particularly close.

There were significant differences in the different homes. We both had to learn what was acceptable at the respective households. In Somerset, for example, we all read while eating, but in Brighton, Justina was told off for doing the same thing. Dad and Jan's, was a modern, ultra-tidy, vegetarian household with central heating, a phone, carpets etc. On the farm in Somerset, it was a rougher, less well-off, messier lifestyle. We didn't have carpets or central heating, there were animals nearby and meat on the table. Marta became adept at taking the innards out of rabbits, chickens, whilst I watched with a mixture of fascination and revulsion.

Dad had decided to become vegetarian in 1959, shortly after he had married Marta. Marta was enthusiastic about vegetarianism at first but lost interest completely after the split. Vegetarianism became symbolic of their separation.

Justina and I found ourselves caught in the middle which made life

A New Man

difficult for the two of us. Colin would cruelly mock Justina for not eating the Sunday roast and Marta said to me, 'Don't you dare ever become vegetarian!' It would be a long-lasting test of our loyalties.

At school, I got on well with the other kids, but I didn't learn much. I'd ask for homework as I was keen to learn but was told I couldn't have any. When it came to the 11+ exam later, Colin and Marta omitted to even let me know they had put me in for it which meant I wasn't prepared. When I came out of the test room my cheeks were burning hot, my head was heavy and I was spinning. Having never had homework or even a test or any sort, I was in a state of shock. I failed, unsurprisingly.

The school bus was a different sort of education. I carelessly copied the way the older girls on the bus spoke once and called Marta 'a bitch' in an argument. She was livid and whacked me hard more than a few times. 'Don't you dare ever, ever use that word!' she shouted at me. I never did use the word again. Another time, I saw an older girl rush off the school bus in tears with her bra off and blouse nearly falling off; a group of boys were laughing as she fled. I was disturbed by her distress, caused by them having assaulted her.

Celyn showed me some photos of women's breasts in a newspaper he'd found and we laughed together but I felt strange because now, aged ten, I was starting to feel uncomfortable about the differences between girls and boys and the fact that clearly, physically I was not a boy.

I thought my life would be just so much more straightforward if only I had been born a boy. I was treated like a boy most of the time and I felt I was a boy. I stuffed my pants with socks and other items and it felt good pretending that I had a penis. I even simulated sexual intercourse with a large rag doll Marta had made me, which was the same height as me.

I continued to try to be as boyish as possible and I was disappointed when strangers referred to me as a girl. Once an older boy wanted to play a game which involved hitting each other with rolled up magazines. I tried my hardest to hit him but he hit me very hard. I gave up and then even started crying as well - I was annoyed with myself, I had failed this test of masculinity and failed it twice by crying.

At least in terms of outside appearance my body at this stage wasn't that different to boy's. I had a flat chest and was quite strong. I even had passionate relationships with girls from school and we would kiss and give each other love bites. Sometimes they would say they were 'just practising.'

To me, this was the real thing. The times I had with one girlfriend were very exciting, we played many sexual games. One game was in the barn full of stepped straw bales giving the appearance of rows of seats around a flat area where we pretended we were in a swimming pool-she started having difficulties in the water and my role was to dive in, save her, take her clothes off and ravish her. But then things started to change. Another girl I got close to pushed me away on her bed, when I put my arm around her and said disgustedly to me, 'You're not a boy!' I was humiliated. Girls were becoming interested in boys and the hard truth was, I wasn't one.

What was worse was that boys were now becoming interested in me. Marta often had school boys come and visit us and one, Michael who was 14 years old tried to play sexual games with me. We were upstairs one Sunday afternoon when he got my hand and placed it on his crotch. I moved it away instantly. I picked up a pillow and chucked it at him preferring a pillow fight to anything sexual but he put my hand on his crotch again. I managed to get free from his grasp and go downstairs. I told him that I was only ten and far too young, but frustratingly he just said, 'That's okay, I like them young.'

I thought that I was supposed to like his attention. I put up with him kissing me. It didn't repulse me, but I didn't particularly like it much either. I didn't get the same thrill as I had with the girlfriends I'd had. I told Marta I was fed up with him, but I didn't tell her what he was up to with me because I felt embarrassed. I knew I much preferred being with girls, which I was now learning wasn't acceptable.

I had passionate feelings towards girls and I had to work out how I could be, how I would fit in with my friends and at school, and there was the problem of how to deal with boys like Michael, but before I

Λ New Man

could start to work anything out, there was another upheaval. I was getting used to the new secondary school and was halfway through the first year when we moved again, this time much further away, to the north of England.

4

To Yorkshire

It was pouring with rain the day we moved to Yorkshire in March in 1977. The removal lorry had loaded up and was about to leave when the driver asked Colin how long it would take us to get there. We were due to drive up separately in the Morris Minor van with all the plants and wine bottles; Colin replied, 'About nine hours.'

There were so many signs that this move was going to be a disaster and it started from day one. It was obvious that they would arrive long before us but no plan was made. When we arrived after the arduous journey we were presented with a distressing sight: all our stuff had been dumped on the ground. It was raining hard and much of it was getting wet and damaged. The caravan we were to live in had been put right next to a rubbish tip and we had no running water and no functioning toilet.

Marta and Colin had been looking for somewhere to get their own farm. A friend of theirs said they knew someone called Alastair, an ex-army man who owned a private boarding school and had some unused land next to the school grounds. So, there was a possibility of setting up a farm on this land and it was decided to set up the dreamed-for Jersey dairy farm there. The private school was located about nine miles from York, far away from shops and facilities. We had to go into the school buildings to use a toilet and washing facilities. I had to endure the posh private school kids looking down their noses at me.

After nearly a year, the caravan was finally moved away from the rubbish tip and into an orchard. This was an improvement though we still didn't have running water so we were using holes in the ground for toilets which was freezing in the cold Yorkshire winter.

As we had moved to a different education authority, I had to go through yet another torturous selection process. This meant more time

A New Man

off school whilst waiting. After three months off school I was allocated to go to the local secondary modern as I had failed again. Colin didn't care which school I went to but Marta objected and decided to try and get me into one of the comprehensives. In York at the time all the schools were either grammar or secondary moderns apart from three comprehensives on the outskirts.

Marta managed to get me into a good comprehensive through a combination of having the audacity to ask and sheer good fortune. She turned up unannounced for an interview for a teaching job. The headmaster agreed to meet her and he was kind but warned her that there had already been 200 applicants. Marta gave up on the idea of the job immediately and instead pointed at me, as I had come along too, and asked if I could be accepted instead. I think the headmaster was just so taken aback that he just agreed there and then and that's how I ended up going to a good school but one miles away, right on the other side of York.

In the days leading up to leaving school in Somerset, I had felt quite popular. Everyone said nice things, even those I wasn't particularly friends with, and they said they'd write and keep in touch. No one wrote and no one kept in touch. Celyn came up and visited once which was good but being so far away, the friendship severed as did all the others.

In Yorkshire and saddled with a southern accent, I had to start again and try and make new friends. I felt odd and isolated at school. At home, living miles away from York, and encapsulated within a private boarding school, there was also little chance of me finding a suitable friend. For a while I tried to be friends with the school cook's daughter but we had nothing in common. She was obsessed with the TV programme 'Charlie's Angels' and hated sport whereas I wanted to play football and have adventures. I craved companionship like I'd had with Celyn.

The boys from the private school were unfriendly and arrogant. Marta began to teach art at the private school to help with the financial situation but they were rude to my mum which made me angry.

To Yorkshire

They looked down at her because they said they were paying her to teach them. When I was in the swimming pool on my own, they threw stones at me, hence I kept out of their way as much as possible. There were lots of facilities at the private school: lawn tennis, swimming, table tennis and horse riding but without anyone to join me, they were as good as useless to me.

Living so far away, I had to be out of the house by 7.30am to take the car journey and two bus rides to get to school in time. On the way back, after the second bus had dropped me off, I had to dial home from the phone box, wait for it to ring twice and then put the phone down and wait for a lift. This was to save the telephone costs. I would hope that it was Marta coming to collect me, it usually was, but sometimes it would be Colin, and I'd be uncomfortable and the conversation would be stilted during the drive back. Sometimes a lift wasn't possible at all if it was late and I'd have to walk the mile back in the pitch-black dark. The bus journeys were expensive which made me feel guilty as Marta paid for all the transport costs out of her own money as it had been her decision for me to go to a good school.

One Christmas I asked Marta why there was supposed to be a Father Christmas and not a Mother Christmas. She said it was because the father figure was viewed as the provider. This didn't make sense to me. Marta paid the school travel costs for me, she gave me pocket money, bought me especially smart and decent clothes for school and drove me everywhere in her own car she had bought. I developed respect for women who had their own source of income and some semblance of independence. I was determined never to be dependent on anyone.

If moving to another part of the country and a new school wasn't awful enough, next I had to cope with the onset of periods. I was an early starter, getting them at age eleven. Marta showed me how to use sanitary towels but I found wearing them awful; they were uncomfortable, and a hassle to change. I struggled with all the female paraphernalia as I had not long been given a bra to start wearing as well. It was stressful and the straps around my back were uncomfortable and restrictive. I failed to see why anyone would be delighted in having

A New Man

reached womanhood.

Justina visited and showed me how to use tampons, which was a big improvement. I shaved my under-arm hair for the first time too, though no one warned me that it wasn't a good idea to put deodorant on straight afterwards-it stung so viciously that I resolved never to shave under my arms again.

With puberty, I had inevitably started to look less like a boy. Although I still had visible arm muscles, Colin remarked that shop keepers and other people would soon stop referring to me as a boy. I asked why and he replied, 'Because your tits are showing!' The emphasised word 'tits' stabbed me but I swallowed, didn't say anything and hoped he hadn't seen how much he had upset me.

It took me two years to be accepted in the school, but I did eventually settle in. It was decided at school early on by the others in my class to call me Charlie which I had no objection too and it felt friendly. 'David' had been left behind in Somerset. My main overriding objective was to be accepted again. I didn't have space to think about my preferred masculine identity whilst trying to fit in to the new school.

Hockey was substituted for football and I became good at it which helped me make friends. Later I played for York Area under-16 team and Colin came and watched me play once, though disappointingly Marta never did. The PE teachers warned me though that my leg muscles were getting far too big playing sport which wouldn't be attractive when I got older. They also said that Martina Navratilova was far too muscly, whereas I thought she was great and powerful.

I began to enjoy school, especially spending time with people my own age but I dreaded coming home as the atmosphere at home was tense and unpleasant. In the caravan, it was cramped and there was a lot of anxiety about the farm. Alastair would drop in regularly and say the farm wasn't making enough money. Colin didn't manage at all well under the strain. Colin and Marta both worked extremely hard, but the idea of enjoying the animals and the countryside went out the window. Marta tried to resist this but she wasn't even accepted as a business partner by Alistair who was a fairly typical upper class sexist man and she was side-lined with Colin not bothering to support her. The farm business partnership was therefore set up between Colin and Alistair only.

The profit margin for the farm business was the only concern. Colin became resentful of anyone else not working as hard as him and he had no social skills. He barked at everyone, even shocked visitors during dinner, demanding silence for the weather forecast and then at 9pm sharp he would announce he had to turn in and that everyone had to be completely quiet not to disturb him. I was embarrassed to be associated with him.

I tried to avoid working much on the farm but I was always getting called to lend a hand. Colin would say 'Grab that, would you?' or 'Go and get that, would you?' it grated on me that he never said please. I had to work on the farm sometimes of course, I couldn't avoid it. I often had to squeegee up the cow dung in the yard but I was rarely permitted to do more enjoyable things like drive the tractor. On one memorable occasion, I was given permission to drive it, first with a trailer and then without. The tractor shot off without the trailer going at some speed, that was great fun. The only other time Colin offered me the chance to drive the tractor was when Dad was just about to leave after a visit, so I was distracted and didn't give him a proper hug goodbye.

Once after days of non-stop rain, I was woken up at four in the morning as there was a serious risk of all the cows drowning as they were stranded on an island that was gradually disappearing under the rising water of the river, which had breached its banks. It was dark and we carried torches to see where the cows were to try and rescue them. There was a lot of shouting in the darkness. We managed it in the end by putting a rope around one cow that was considered a leader of the rest, and then with all our might, we pushed and pulled her through the water which was then only about two or three feet deep. When she had made it to dry land the others followed. This was a rare occasion when Marta, Colin and I managed to come together, faced with an emergency.

In the evenings, after school, I had to mix up the powdered milk for

A New Man

the young gorgeous Jersey calves and then try and make them drink it. This involved sticking my two fore fingers in the powdered substitute milk and trying to get them to suck on my fingers and draw up the milk at the same time. Inevitably my fingers would get chewed. They were heartbreakingly beautiful but I found it so frustrating that they wouldn't drink and instead gnawed my fingers that sometimes I gave up and threw the milk over them, then I felt awful.

I was given a bullock of my own. I named him Sam but lost interest quickly because he would be going to go the slaughter house. The idea was that I would pay for the food and after he was sold for slaughter, I would make a profit and this was supposed to endear me to farm life. From my experience, there wasn't much hope for animals as I saw they had an awful time on farms. Because of this and Colin's attitude, I had little enthusiasm for farming.

Colin wanted me to be completely immersed in the farm but I didn't like working for him one iota especially as Colin started to have help from one of Alistair's sons, Timothy. I was quite proud of my strong arm muscles but there was no way I could compete with this boy, who was well past puberty and about three years older than me. Timothy could lift four bales of hay whereas I could lift only two. I'd grab the orange plastic twine that held the heavy hay bales together, it hurt my hands, and I'd grasp the two twines together for each bale and then straining to lift, carry one on each side of me with them swinging and scratching my legs.

Timothy would stride ahead with four bales smiling at my lesser ability. Colin praised him continually in front of me and Marta and then even started paying him. I asked Colin how much he was paying him and was told sternly to mind my own business. My contribution wasn't worth as much but I wasn't even thanked. Colin simply thought I was useless and said so regularly.

Home life was miserable for both Marta and me. We fantasised about leaving the misery of the farm and researched where we would like to move to. I got a map of England out and we thought about moving to the seaside together, just the two of us. We got quite interested

To Yorkshire

in Great Yarmouth. Marta seemed keen and serious too. We looked at the facilities there. I thought it was a real possibility and was excited about it but it was only ever going to be a dream. We also fantasised about just going away for a holiday. We both were enthusiastic about going to Blackpool but never made it. The infrequent family holidays stopped after we moved to Yorkshire. (We'd been to Northumberland, to France and to Wales.)

I started to eat for comfort and consequently I put on a lot of weight. This meant Colin called me fat as well as lazy and useless. Colin was skinny. He could get through huge piles of food on his plate without it making any difference. I resented cooking as I saw this as a purely a service provided by women for men and I vowed never to learn to cook so that I would never be forced to be in the position of serving a man like I saw Marta do for Colin, day in day out with little gratitude. Visitors to the farm including boys my age also expected me to serve them because I was a girl. I found it infuriating but Marta just told me to accept it and put up with it.

Marta was, however, very encouraging and said I could be anything I wanted to be, even Prime Minister. This was the polar opposite of Colin's opinion of me. Colin and I had grown to despise each other. At dinner, I'd put one hand on the side of my face and read so that I didn't have to look at him. He didn't care. We all used to read at the table anyway so this made it easier to avoid looking at him. As if to emphasise the order of the family hierarchy, the kitchen chairs bore a direct resemblance to our relative positions. Colin had the largest throne looking chair. Marta had a smaller Queen-like looking chair and I had one of the much smaller pawn-like chairs.

I was so angry at his condescending, sneering attitude one evening whilst he was sat in the chair wiggling his toes smugly, I could not contain my seething hatred for him any longer and I lunged at him. This resulted in both of us grappling with each other on the floor and Marta shouting in alarm at Colin to leave me alone, even though it was me who had started it. Colin in fact never hit me once but rows became even more frequent, sometimes with cups being thrown at each other.

A New Man

The next Christmas, after Colin had handed me his present. I handed it back to him without opening it, saying, 'I don't want a present from you.' It didn't seem right accepting a present from someone I despised. He was offended and in the end, after protestations from Marta, I took it. It was another clock. His presents to me were always clocks or watches as a reminder to be punctual or something boringly practical for my bike. Colin's wrapped his presents in newspapers, neatly symbolic of his meanness and a contrast to my dad's presents which were wrapped in bright coloured paper and with pictured or metallic coloured tape.

I found out that during these unhappy years Colin had been propositioning nearly every female friend of my mum's. He even tried to have sex with Dad's partner Jan. She said he had come into the room, where she was in bed having a lie-in and that he had started undressing saying she'd been giving him the eye. Jan promptly told him where to go. Undoubtedly, he would have been unfaithful, probably many times. Later he told Marta he was waiting until I was old enough before leaving her. I wish he hadn't waited.

5

The Life Saver: Punk

The one good thing about living miles away from York and even further from my school was that this was the perfect excuse for not having a boyfriend. I was now thirteen and at school girls were demanding to know why not. I had no interest whatsoever in boys in that way but I felt pressure to be like everyone else, so my response was to say that it was difficult meeting anyone because I lived so far away. It seemed to satisfy people.

I had no desire to put make-up on and wear clothes for the sole purpose of making myself appear attractive to boys. At school, I'd try and wear trousers as much as possible and was one of the few girls that chose to wear the school blazer and tie. I liked wearing them, it made me feel more like one of the boys.

I was in the main shopping street in York one Saturday afternoon when a school friend bumped into me. I was wearing my usual unisex clothes, just jeans, a baggy brown jumper and boots and I had no make-up on. She was surprised to see that that I was carrying a bag from a trendy girls' fashion shop. However, I had only picked up some coat hangers so when I showed her those she laughed and said, 'I thought you'd bought something from the shop.' I was not offended; I had no interest in buying girly fashionable clothes.

There was, however, quite a lot of pressure to conform to being feminine. When I was visiting in Brighton, Dad's partner, Jan, took me on a shopping trip. She bought me stilettos, a big turquoise knotted T shirt and black shimmer leggings. I know she meant well and I did appreciate the attention but when I wore the clothes and shoes at the local disco I found it unbearable. This just wasn't me.

After sitting on the side for some time, a boy asked me to dance. I obliged, all the time wondering what on earth I was doing. I felt like I

A New Man

was acting and acting badly. We attempted a slow dance. Every part of me wished I was somewhere else. I hated how those clothes made me feel. For some women appearing sexy might bring a sense of power, whereas for me, the very last thing I wanted to do was to invite sexual attention. Even though I wanted to fit in and be like the others, I felt a fraud. I walked out of the hall straight after the dance and realised that I could never wear clothes like that again.

Not long after this torturous experience, I was rescued from the pressure to be attractive to boys, by punk entering my world. The Sex Pistols, their hits 'Anarchy in the UK' and 'God Save the Queen' and their 'fuck everything and everybody' attitude hit me like a thunder bolt. This was me: disappointed and angry with life's restrictions.

I finally heard a voice that I could completely identify with, angry young people like me, people who had had enough of the pressure to conform to being gentlemanly or ladylike. Punks wanted a different life to the normal oppressive world of school, work and family life. I certainly didn't have any positive feelings towards the notion of family. In fact, the word 'family' stuck in my throat. I didn't feel alone anymore with this disillusionment and that felt good.

With punk, I could jettison the feminine teenage girl image that I never convincingly fitted into. Now I wore Dr Marten boots, black drainpipe jeans, baggy shirts and a donkey jacket. I made a t-shirt with zips in it. I spiked my hair up using the cheap punk method of sugar and water. Very occasionally I'd put on black lipstick as a concession but I only ever wore trousers and boots. I would have given anything for a black leather jacket but at this Marta put her foot down and insisted that I couldn't have one even if I saved up for it. I couldn't fathom why she objected so much. Perhaps it was just too much a symbol of rebellion.

Punk rescued me. This was far more than just music. Punk was about being an individual and I agreed with the statements that everyone deserved respect and that no one should have to follow the imposed route of girlfriend/boyfriend dating, career, marriage and children. I was inspired and felt that I had found a comfortable iden-

The Life Saver: Punk

tity and one that I could be accepted in without having to wear skirts. Although there were some punk girls who wore loads of make-up and mini-skirts with fishnet tights, many didn't. I didn't have to put up with questions about not being a typical teenage girl; people just assigned me to the 'punk' category. No one said I wasn't being feminine when dancing. No one said I shouldn't pogo or dance roughly with boys and I could hold my own physically in these dances and partly because of this I was left alone.

I looked out for punks on Saturdays when I cycled the nine miles into York and I joined a gang of punks. They were all older than me, I was 13 but looked older, they were aged between 15 and 19. Most of the punks had leather jackets or donkey jackets and they all had spiky dyed punk hair styles including Mohicans. We hung out either in the rock and roll greasy spoon cafe or in the Theatre Royal café, stretching out cups of tea for hours until we were asked to leave.

One young woman in the gang was a Siouxsie Sioux lookalike. She was part-Indian, part-Irish; her name was Colleen and she was stunningly attractive with jet black spiky hair. She copied Siouxsie's make-up perfectly. I developed a crush on her. Marta sensed that I really liked her a lot and I pointed Colleen out to her once in admiration and Marta didn't seem to mind at all. She could tell I was happy to be in the punk gang. It helped that a daughter of Ruth, a friend of Marta's, was in the gang too.

My very first gig involved skiving from school. I went with Liz, a cool mature-acting friend from my class, to see 'The Jam' in Bridlington. Bridlington was about 40 miles from York so we had to leave school early to get there in time. Without much money, we had no choice but to hitchhike. Two middle aged blokes picked us up in a battered Ford Cortina. Liz and I both looked at each other uneasily after we accepted their offer of a lift and got in. They were both heavy smokers and we also accepted cigarettes from them. It was farcical with the four of us all smoking in the car as you could hardly see anything.

The driving was erratic. They said that they had just come out of prison, whether that was true or not, we never found out. Fortunately,

A New Man

they turned out to be safe and reliable and they even waited for the gig to finish and drove us back again to York.

Predictably, Colin, a classical music lover and former hippy, despised punk. He considered it unsophisticated and devoid of any merit. He told me I looked ugly and disgusting when I was on my way out once, dressed in a punk style. I was wearing black PVC trousers, boots and a mohair top, spiked up hair and I also had black lipstick on. This hurtful comment was typical of him, though it still affected me. I played my punk records upstairs in my room and he played his classical records downstairs and we would try to drown each other out. Marta on the other hand liked to be interested in what I was interested in and was helpful. When there was a weekend punk festival in Leeds, she drove down in her Morris van so that we could sleep in it overnight on the Saturday.

One band grabbed me and energised me like no other, this was an anarchist, vegetarian, anti-war, feminist band called CRASS. Much of it sounded similar to the raw angry punk sounds of the time but the words were pro peace and they mocked macho men. One of their albums which featured only the women in CRASS was outstanding and I found the words poetic and clever. For example, the opening words to 'Poison in a Pretty Pill' written by one of the women in CRASS, Joy de Vivre, were:

> Your tactile eyes running over glossy paper
> Printed on with tactile lies of glaze and gauze
> They say 'forget yourself, adorn with this disguise'
> This womanhood of smooth and tampered whores
> Let me warn you of their cold sensitivity
> They'll have you gathered in a trap of glass
> Is your reflection all that you will recognise?
> That cruel lie will stare you in the face
> Wrapped up in a haze and flow of bridal gown
> They tell your lover he must hold a gun
> You're the pornographic reassurance he's a man

The Life Saver: Punk

> They deal with flesh, incarcerate with rags
> Red lips, shimmer-silk and body-bags
> Hairless legs against the blistered napalm burn
> I want to rape the substance of your downy hair
> In that mist a gutted child fights for air.

Marta was impressed and was convinced that their records would be worth a lot one day so she bought all their records. I was in complete awe of them.

As drugs didn't appeal to me, (Marta's anti-drug influence was strong) I liked that they didn't idolise drink or drugs as so many bands did and they instead sung about dope heads being arrogant and superior. CRASS sold their records cheaper than everyone else and they avoided standard marketing and publicity. To me they were the real deal; they lived their lives as they wanted to, not how music marketing executives told them how to. I admired them and defended them forcefully.

Listening to the words sung by CRASS and other punk groups, made me re-evaluate my thoughts on the army too. Up until becoming a punk I had been thinking about joining the army, (despite not being able to be a royal marine and having to wear skirts) but I started to think individualism and fighting the notion of war itself was more important.

At school a boy in my year mocked and taunted me by singing the CRASS song 'shaved women' in a snide disparaging way. I was personally insulted as if he'd insulted me and I pushed him hard against the wall lifting him up by his collar, he didn't retaliate and said he didn't hit girls. That just annoyed me more as he obviously didn't think I was of equal status.

One day when crossing the park to school, a trainee student teacher from France I was walking with happened to casually mention to me that she was going to see CRASS that evening. I stopped dead in my tracks. I wanted to see CRASS more than anything, so I tentatively asked if I could go with her. She said 'Yeah, sure.' I don't think she real-

A New Man

ised that I was only thirteen, I did act older but it was clear that I was still at school. I was beside myself with excitement. That afternoon I skipped another class and went with her to hitch-hike all the way from York to Liverpool. I knew I needed to let my mum know as soon as possible that I would be late home.

A few hours later we arrived at a house in Liverpool where some friends of hers were staying. It was quite basic: no carpets, not much furniture and no phone. It might have been a squat. I said I had to go outside to find a phone box but then we all started to make our way to the gig. I quickly looked around and ran up and down the streets nearby but it was no use, the two phone boxes I eventually found were both out of order. Time was moving on and I came to the conclusion that at this rate, I might not even get to see the band I'd made such an effort to see, so I made the decision to abandon the search for a working phone box until later and went with everyone to the gig.

Inside the small venue, instead of a big stage highlighting the band the band members were all dressed in black with barely any stage lighting, there was a film shown throughout the set behind the band which included collated snippets of war and other political imagery. The atmosphere was charged. One of the friends asked me if I wanted a drink, I didn't know what to ask for and he assumed that I would want a pint of beer so I had my first ever pint. I felt exhilarated to be there and I became slightly tipsy.

There was just the nagging awkward feeling that I hadn't managed to find a phone box to let Marta know where I was but there was nothing I could do but accept it. After the gig, it looked like we were going to stay over and I explained that I had to get back to York. I gave up looking for a working phone box and thought the best thing to do was to get back to York as soon as possible. At 5am the following morning we hitched-hiked back to York. I arrived at school only about an hour late. I thought I'd done well getting back so quickly, but then the Deputy Head hauled me out of the French class I was in and asked me where I'd been.

'I went to Liverpool to see the band CRASS,' I explained.

'Well I certainly hope it was worth it,' she replied ominously.

I was taken straight to the Headmasters office. There was now a new headmaster and he was unfriendly and arrogant. He looked at me with utter disgust and said, 'What a selfish beast, you are.' I was offended and taken back by his over the top reaction. I wanted to explain that I often went to punk gigs with my mum's acceptance.

Marta and Colin arrived at school, Colin attempted to look serious wearing a suit but it didn't work as he was wearing cowboy boots at the same time. I wished he wasn't associated with me. He looked ridiculous. In the headmaster's room with Marta and Colin I got another telling off. Then we all went to the police station for me to have another grilling. The policeman was fierce and he said that I had been really stupid and then he asked me if I had taken any drugs, he said he could have me tested to check that I hadn't. The irony was that I had seen a band opposed to drugs. I started to cry, which seemed to be what he wanted as he said, 'Well at least you're crying now,' and he toned down his onslaught.

It was true that the two of us had taken a risk and, as Colin said sneeringly, that two men could have easily held us both down and raped us but in my head my defence was that I had been introduced to hitchhiking by Colin in the first place. In any case, if I'd managed to find a phone box that worked then I wouldn't be in this situation at all. I felt I was being unjustly punished.

I didn't understand why suddenly people were so bothered about what I was getting up to and where I was. No one seemed to care normally. Marta removed of all my records until the end of term as an additional punishment and the school head ordered that I did voluntary work one afternoon every week. This consisted of me having to visit a psychiatric hospital for the elderly which was an unsettling and troubling experience. I wasn't prepared for what I saw. I was put on a ward for elderly women. My tasks were to help mentally disturbed women drink tea from a beaker and be company to them. They'd talk but they didn't talk sense or they would come out with wild statements.

'I used to be the Mayoress of York you know,' garbled a 90-year-old

A New Man

woman, in-between me giving her sips of tea from the baby beaker cup. I didn't know whether to believe her or not. I found it desperately sad, it was as if all these older women had been abandoned by their families. They were all very sedate and didn't appear to be a problem to anyone other than probably needing help with personal care. I tried making things more exciting and for one woman and I gave her a high-speed trip in her wheelchair running down the corridor as fast as I could. She seemed to enjoy it.

The atmosphere deteriorated further at home with worsening arguments. Stressed by it all, I started pulling my hair out. I didn't realise I was doing this at first, but I had started to twist the hair around my fingers and then pull it. This created a large band of baldness on my forehead which I then had to try and hide. When I was running in a school race, I accidentally revealed the patch to all those watching. I meant to keep my head down carefully for the entire race, then at the final 200 metres I forgot and I looked up and my hair flared back revealing the strip of baldness across my forehead. People watching the race looked shocked but it was so shameful they didn't say anything at all to me.

Marta was worried about the worsening bald patch on my head. When we were getting dinner ready she said, 'Perhaps I ought to take you to see a psychiatrist.'

I quickly fired back, 'You'd better not!' in a defiant tone. I was absolutely terrified at that suggestion. I was adamant that I wouldn't see anyone and she dropped the idea.

After arguments with Colin I ran away many times but I didn't stay away for long. We'd fight over how much work I should do on the farm. I hated feeding the calves their powdered milk, and complained I had school homework to do. We had another physical tussle over this, I didn't want to feed the calves and I used the excuse of homework. He backed down but ultimately, he had no respect for me and likewise I had none for him. What always brought me back to the farm was that Marta would get so upset. I'd phone her from York to reassure her and she would be crying asking me to go back so I went back for her as I felt too awful causing her pain, I couldn't bear it.

The Life Saver: Punk

Just before my sixteenth birthday, everything changed as both Marta and I had to pack up and leave the farm.

6

Joining the Lesbian Community

It began when a Dutch agricultural student came to stay at the farm. The husband of one of Marta's friends was Dutch and had asked Colin and Marta if they would consider taking a student on for farm work experience. Colin and Marta received a letter from this Dutch student. I remember the letter in Colin's hands when he was trying to make out the signature. 'It looks like Oscar' he said, and they assumed the student was male. It was late spring of 1981, I was fifteen and coming up to my end of school exams. I had done okay in the mocks but after the student arrived, my life turned upside down.

Oscar turned out to be Ciska, a tall, blonde, grinning, physically strong woman, who was enthusiastic about farming and who wanted to impress and work hard. The plan was that she would sleep in a separate caravan next to the farm. Ciska was 17, just a year and a few months older than me. Colin tumbled head over heels for her and they fell in love. They were rudely indiscreet.

A few weeks later, Marta returned late one day to find a strange atmosphere, the candles low and the two of them sharing a bottle of wine. That night, Colin got up from the bed he was sharing with Marta and told her he was going back to bed with Ciska in the caravan.

Marta phoned the Samaritans distraught but the woman on the other end wasn't any help and just blamed foreign women. This was the second time my mum's husbands had fallen for young female students and I was beginning to think badly of men and their selfishness.

Colin was adamant. He had fallen in love with Ciska and that was all he cared about. Soon afterwards Marta and I left the farm. She drove us to York and we stayed with her best friend Ruth, who she had met from an art class she had been attending. That evening the three of us sat at the dining room table discussing the awful situation.

'I am so angry, I want to burn that caravan down, preferably with the two of them in it,' I said. In my mind, I could see the flames burning the curtains and then as it took hold, the roar of the fire ruthlessly destroying the nightmare of the infidelity happening in that caravan. Ruth and Marta looked at each other and then at me, they could see my seething fury.

They tried to reason with me,

'Now that's not a good idea, is it! It would be disastrous and you'd end up in prison' Marta said, 'It would be the end of your life.'

If the caravan had been easier to get to, with less time to think, I may well have done it. I didn't particularly care about the consequences at that point.

We stayed with Ruth and her husband Hugh for a couple of weeks longer. It was a refuge for us. I was there for my 16th birthday in July and we tried to make the best of the situation, a cake was bought.

After the school term had ended and all the exams finished. Marta decided to visit other friends so we embarked on a road trip. First, we stayed in Northampton then Marta wanted us to go to Holland to visit Justina where she was now living since leaving Brighton. I had to get a passport, so I had my photo taken in the post office in the middle of Northampton. On seeing the photo, Marta said I looked awful out loud. It was true I did look awful. I looked dishevelled, unkempt, in a state and I had a thoroughly miserable expression.

I ran out of the post office crying. I started running down a road. I very nearly decided to run and run far away for good but I didn't know Northampton at all, I didn't know where to go. Dejected, I turned back and met up with Marta again in the post office. She was relieved I'd come back. Then we travelled on to Holland.

Justina hadn't yet properly settled in Amsterdam. She was living in a squat and offered what support she could. We then drove up to Alkmaar, in the north of Holland, and visited the same people who had organised for Ciska to come to the farm. But then, as if things couldn't get worse, one of Marta's friends from the art group died in a car crash with her husband and their two children. This was another devastat-

A New Man

ing emotional bomb for Marta. I felt Marta's pain and offered what comfort I could.

We returned to England some weeks later to the farm to collect important stuff. Marta instructed to me to go to my room, and collect what I wanted. I didn't have long, only about half an hour. When we went inside the house, the setting that met us made me want to throw up. The place was unusually tidy and clean, whereas before I was the only one who tidied up, there were Dutch clogs and traditional blue Dutch tiles on the walls hung up as ornaments; on the table, there was poetry and writings lying around of how much Colin loved Ciska. I felt sick. I ran upstairs to my room and tried to decide which things were the most important. Clothes were important obviously, and I grabbed a couple of my favourite books, such as Roots. But I couldn't take everything that was important to me and it was so rushed. I didn't have time to think carefully or reflect. I didn't know that was my only chance to retrieve my possessions.

Where were we going to go? Marta said I needed to be sorted out first. It seemed to make sense that I stayed on at school in York for some continuity but I hadn't done well enough to stay on in sixth form. My mum managed to persuade the headmaster to let me stay on to re-take some exams and start French and Sociology at A level. He warned me sternly that I would have to study hard.

The problem was that I needed somewhere to stay. We visited some places together but they all seemed so horrible. One was a small ugly pink bedsit with an unfriendly landlady. I didn't want to be on my own in some awful bedsit. We were on the street, after visiting yet another horrible bedsit when Marta lost her temper with me. Frustrated with the mess we were both in, and she turned to me and shouted, 'Just find somewhere on your own and sort yourself out!' I felt stranded. Marta apologised. The pressure was all getting too much for both of us.

The next day we passed a café and I saw a sign in the window that said, 'Lodger wanted- apply within' and I pointed it out to Marta.

'This looks hopeful and it doesn't look too expensive,' I said.

'It's certainly worth a try,' Marta said.

Joining the Lesbian Community

We walked inside and met the advertiser- a woman in the cafe. The woman, Kathryn, sat down with us both and we had a cup of coffee. She was fine about me moving in; her one concern was that she didn't want to be responsible for me. Marta reassured her that she wouldn't be.

Kathryn turned out to live right next door to a friend of Marta's and the house was within walking distance to my school past the park so it all seemed suitable. I moved in just a week before sixth form was due to start.

Dad came up to visit me belatedly and he suggested that I move to Worthing where he had moved to with his partner and their daughter who was now six years old. But that didn't seem right although it was nice to be considered. I'd just got it organised to move into this place and got things sorted with school. He suggested that I go to his art college, but I didn't have a strong interest in art. It would be another upheaval. On another level, I felt it would be a betrayal to Marta as if she had failed if I moved in with him. I knew I had to keep things together.

As a lodger, lots of things were new to me; I had never even written out a cheque before and I wasn't good at cooking of course. However, now that I was an official single parent family though a one-person family, really, I was entitled to free school meals which was invaluable.

Colin found out that I was lodging and despatched a black and white TV for me. But there wasn't any room for a telly. There was only room for a single bed and a desk. I perched it precariously on top of the desk. In the small narrow white bedroom with high windows, I tried to feel at home and be grown up but in truth I cried regularly at night. Ruth said not to tell Marta. I was so upset at how things had turned out and angry at the terrible way Marta had been treated.

Inexplicably, Dad defended Colin saying that he couldn't help falling in love with a 17-year-old but I felt Marta's pain. I wished that Colin had ended it earlier in a more humane manner instead of embarking on an affair right in front of us.

I set about changing all my documentation back to 'Kiss'. It was easy

A New Man

because Colin had never legally adopted me and I had possession of my birth certificate. Soon I had changed every document I had, it was a satisfying, empowering feeling. I thought back to Justina's request to me as a kid, 'Don't forget to ask for your real name back.'

But I had money problems. I wrote a letter to dad showing a list of my outgoing and incoming amounts to demonstrate the shortfall; and that the list didn't even include food or transport. My school friend Jane started stealing the odd can of food from her house for me. Jane was one of the few people who had seen Colin's behaviour first-hand and confirmed for me that he was indeed rude and snide, it hasn't just been from my perspective. So, she understood my predicament and tried to be supportive. Marta sent me money but it wasn't enough; it only paid for the rent and the bills. Marta then asked Dad to help and reluctantly he did. Reluctantly as it had been the agreement that he would look after Justina and Marta would look after me, as I understood it, so I started to receive a bit more but it still wasn't enough.

Then I tried to get additional money from the state but that wasn't approved as I had to prove I'd been completely abandoned by my parents which wasn't the case. Three months after moving, Colin contacted me and started paying a small contribution directly to me by postal order. I wasn't going to say no.

Kathryn was an anxious mother who was a student. She had a little girl aged six and she was doing her best to bring up on her own; however, she had some support from the local community. Every school morning, her daughter would scream and protest about having to go to school, which was intolerable. But the walk to school was luxury, before the journey used to take an hour and a half; now it only took 15 minutes. I was working hard at school to try and take my mind off the events of the past few months.

I could tell from the posters and postcards on the kitchen wall that Kathryn was a feminist. One postcard had a photo of an advertisement with graffiti on it. The advertisement was for a new little car saying, 'Congratulations you have a son' and the graffiti on the advertisement was 'Better luck next time'. This amused me greatly.

Joining the Lesbian Community

I hadn't been there long when I had a strange unpleasant phone call. A man rang, didn't ask who I was and just asked, 'Have you seen Kathryn's clitoris?' I froze and didn't know what to say. Eventually I just replied, 'No' and put the phone down. It turned out that Kathryn had advertised for a lodger also in a York feminist magazine and this is how he got her telephone number. He had obviously made an assumption about her sexuality.

Kathryn did have some friends who were lesbians and she told me that a couple of years back she had in fact had a relationship with a lesbian, Marianne. Marianne was someone I was instantly impressed with. She was sensible and organised. She was handsome. She had a small frame, not overly muscly but she was fit. She drove a big MZ motorbike and she worked in the local gardening nursery often bringing back vegetables for everyone.

Marianne and Kathryn were still friends and so she'd come round often, sometimes to share a joint at the kitchen table. I always enjoyed these visits, though not the smoking. I had no interest in smoking dope but other than that, I wanted to be like her. She lived in an unusual set up, she lived with a friend and the friend's young son but had a lover elsewhere. I admired her and thought she was strong, independent and lived a straightforward peaceful life.

In fact, I discovered that there were quite a few lesbians who looked out for each other on the recently built housing association estate. The houses were very small low rise red brick houses but with walls so thin you felt you knew your neighbour's sex life. Kathryn was now involved with a younger man and she was teased by her lesbian friends about having a toy boy. At night, I had to put up with a lot of groaning and banging of the headboard.

I had male friends at school but they were just friends and nothing else, we'd share punk records and play table football. I was not interested in having a boyfriend in the slightest, I was only attracted to girls, plus I identified with women like Marianne.

Before I left the farm, I had been on a week's visit to London mainly to see the punk artist Toyah with a school friend who was also into

A New Man

punk, Kristin. In London, I had tried to put my arm round her after a night out but she had abruptly told me to 'fuck off' – She was blunt but clear. I was saddened because I liked her a lot. Kristin had long auburn/copper coloured hair, she was slim and wore fashionable punky clothes plus she was very clever. The response may have been the same had I been a boy, of course, but I couldn't help thinking that I might have at least been considered if I'd been male.

So, with all this evidence that I was attracted to girls, it really did seem that the reason for this was that I was a lesbian. It didn't occur to me that I could be transsexual although I remember being fascinated and feeling compassion for 'Julia,' the transsexual woman who transitioned from male to female on a BBC documentary entitled 'George and Julia'. If there had been a female to male version, maybe I would have thought about it earlier. As it was, the lesbian category seemed to fit best. There was also a belief that a woman who was male in appearance or behaviour was a lesbian as well. Although this didn't correspond with the vast majority of lesbians I met. I just thought I was just one of the few masculine appearing lesbians.

I kept my hair short. I never wore make-up, (the punk concession to black lipstick had since been discarded) or jewellery. I only ever wore trousers and boots. I also tried to project a strong 'don't mess with me' image. Although I still liked punk a lot. I felt I had to try and fit into this new lesbian community I found myself part of so I toned down my punk image.

Punk unfortunately wasn't considered lesbian or feminist by my new community. I played a track sung by the women in CRASS about female subjugation, to my new lesbian friends in Kathryn's living room, thinking it would get a good reception, but they didn't get that the words were ironic and they found the sound too raw. Unthinkingly I lent the Dead Kennedys single, 'Too Drunk to Fuck', which I thought was a great energetic song, to a woman I had a crush on but in retrospect it's unsurprising she wasn't impressed with a title like that. When I asked her what she thought of the song, she said she hadn't played it.

Instead the generally accepted 'lesbian feminist' music was stuff like

Joan Armatrading and the Pointer Sisters. Joan Armatrading's beautiful album 'Walk Under Ladders' had not long been released and I couldn't dismiss that music. So, in order to be accepted in this new community, I learned a whole new way of dancing: disco dancing. No more zig zagging diagonally manically into a frenzy and bumping into other punks in the middle of the room. Now I had to learn hip swaying and slow rocking dancing which was very different and not energetic in the slightest.

I went to my first 'women only' disco which felt very odd, as if I had joined a cult. It was just so unusual for there not to be any men there at all. The idea of living life without men appealed though. Instead of fighting and having to demand to be treated equally, you could just be, I reasoned.

I thought back to Colin, to the boy who tried to force me to touch his penis, the man who made an abusive phone call. These men were unpleasant and oppressive. Even my dad, who was better than most, was sexist to a degree and had thought it was fine for Colin to have slept with someone only a year older than me.

The women around me reminded me of men's oppressive sense of superiority, and their neglect of women whilst they were more concerned about their own sexual desires and then of course there was sexual abuse and rape which I heard a lot about though did not personally experience. To compound this, I was living in York at the time of the Yorkshire Ripper who was attacking and killing women around Leeds – which wasn't far away – and there was a lot of tension and fear. The schools even closed early once on a rumour that he was due to attack in York.

Suzanne, a younger lesbian feminist I became close to, told me about the feminist marches she had been on in Leeds. When we were walking through the park together, she demonstrated to me what they'd shouted on the marches, 'What do we want? Men off the streets!' then I joined in, us both enthusiastically singing in rounds 'men off the streets, men off the streets.'

The police at the time were saying the exact opposite, that women

A New Man

should stay indoors and keep off the streets. Responding that men were the problem and should keep off the streets instead was a reasonable and logical statement. These torch-lit demonstrations which took place at night were known as 'Reclaim the Night Marches'

I started going to the York Women's Liberation meetings. I identified with the sentiment of equality of opportunity and agreed with the seven demands of the Women's Liberation Movement which were:

1. Equal pay for equal work
2. Equal education and job opportunities
3. Free contraception
4. Free 24-hour community-controlled childcare
5. Legal and financial independence for women
6. An end to discrimination against lesbians
7. Freedom for all women from intimidation by the threat or use of male violence. An end to the laws, assumptions and institutions which perpetuate male dominance and men's aggression towards women.

When the Pope came to visit York, we were prepared. We got up early and put posters up throughout the centre of York saying, 'If the Pope could get pregnant, abortion would be a sacrament'.

Being part of the lesbian feminist community in York didn't mean only meetings and protests. There was a women's brass band in York too who were in high demand, they played some wonderful cabaret style music and I developed a crush on one of the players. Benefit discos were also a regular feature on the calendar and we all went to the pub often.

Marta meanwhile found a place to buy and moved in. It was a small inexpensive two-up two-down little town house on the corner of a terraced cobbled street. The house was in Colne, an extremely depressed town of high unemployment in Lancashire. Marta kept a room for me there in case I needed it and I was tempted to move in with her. I could have gone to the college there as well but it was now too late as I was enjoying my new-found freedom.

Living as an adult in a welcoming community had its rewards. No having to say where you were going, when you'd be coming back, what you'd be doing. I went to pubs regularly even though I was only sixteen, I was never once challenged on my age and I was treated with a certain amount of respect, finally. I relished the freedom, the convenience of facilities and shops within walking distance and to be surrounded by people. I loved city life and I knew that I would like to move back to London at some point.

A few months later, I moved again, this time to a separatist household in central York where men were not welcome at all, even as guests. One of the women in the house worked in the York co-operative bicycle shop, another studied at the university. I'd met these women in the York women's liberation meetings and I heard that a room would be available soon. The house was bigger and I thought it would be a great idea to move into a separatist household. I felt like it was a step in the right direction, to be around men as little as possible and I wouldn't have to listen to the hassle of getting Kathryn's daughter screaming objection to going to school every morning. This house was much closer to the centre of York and I could still cycle through the university campus to get to school on time easily.

After a few months at this house, one of the women left and Ruth moved into the house from Leicester. Ruth was a similar age to me, so it was good to spend some time with her. She told me that she was in a non-monogamous relationship with another woman called Alice, who was living in Leicester.

From Ruth, I learnt that non-monogamy meant you were involved in more than one relationship at a time. It was politically fashionable in many feminist circles. I didn't fully understand the political theory for it, other than it promoted a 'natural' way to be and was a practical opposition to marital coupledom and so called 'patriarchal ownership' ideals. Most of the York lesbians however, didn't hold this non-monogamy doctrine in high regard and didn't follow it.

I was soon to meet Alice when she came to visit. Alice was taller

A New Man

than me, had blond hair in a bob and had a curvy figure. I was attracted to her as soon as we met and the feeling was mutual.

On her second visit, we became physically intimate but my lust for her was hopelessly immature. We sat on a park bench, I put my arm around her, then she leant over to me and we kissed. This was my first proper kiss as an adult with someone I fancied. It was lovely and it felt good. We kissed for a long time, but then I wanted to move things along. I wanted to touch her large breasts and I tried to lift her blouse up but I couldn't pull it out from her trousers and she got annoyed at my floundering and asked me to stop. I felt like a clumsy teenage boy.

Some weeks later, I went to visit her in Leicester and we went out to the pub. Later that night we went to bed together. We were both drunk. I liked the physical closeness but I felt uncomfortable psychologically when she tried to give me pleasure by going down on me whilst I was sitting on the edge of the bed. I discovered I much preferred giving her pleasure.

She told me she was bisexual, which was practically irrelevant to me until I was in her bedroom once and saw some large men's shoes under the bed. Alice explained she had started sleeping with a man. I was completely aghast. Non-monogamy was clearly just too challenging for me. Alice was now going out with a man as well as one of the women in the house I lived in and there was absolutely no way I felt I could compete with a man. I ended the relationship immediately.

Meanwhile, I was trying to decide what I was going to do after sixth form. At careers events, the sexism was blatant. A male teacher told me that marketing was a good career move for women as there were 'lots of women in marketing' as he put it. Another time a policeman expressed disapproval bordering on disgust when I said I was interested in training to be a motorcyclist police officer. The options seemed very narrow. Therefore, I had no idea of what I was going to do workwise, I just had some general inclinations.

Although I was doing reasonably well at school I was to get caught up in something which superseded everything – 'Greenham Common Women's Peace Camp' This was an anti-nuclear protest camp based directly outside the United States Air force base in Newbury in Berkshire due to take delivery of ground-launched nuclear weapons called 'Cruise Missiles'. Becoming immersed in this made me feel studying was pretty irrelevant when compared to the importance of preventing the likelihood of a limited nuclear war in Europe.

7

Greenham Common Women's Peace Camp

I had read in the newspaper, The Guardian, about a march from Wales against nuclear weapons by some women and that they had stayed outside a nuclear weapons base in Greenham Common and set up a protest peace camp as the media had ignored them. I was very involved in Campaign for Nuclear Disarmament activities. I'd set up York Youth CND with my school friend, Jane, and a Quaker boy and I had been on many large CND demonstrations in central London, making the trip down by coach. Jane was similar to me politically. Her parents had left South Africa due to apartheid so she has strong views on equality and freedom. Jane was also not interested in boyfriends and outraged by sexism, which brought us together.

There was a huge CND demonstration in June 1982 in Central London. It was timed to coincide with Ronald Reagan's visit. Shortly after becoming president, Ronald Reagan had made this statement: 'Yes, there could be a limited nuclear war in Europe'. Things were frightening and urgent, as the deterrence argument, flawed though it was, seemed to have been have been discarded and the US defence secretary was also even saying that the US could survive a nuclear war.

At the end of the rally in Hyde Park. a woman from Greenham spoke about the direct action they were taking at the protest camp and stated that the recent eviction attempt had failed to move them. She spoke of the urgency of the situation and emphasised that sometimes you had to take non-violent direct action to get the issue noticed. She then added that that if anyone wanted to join in an action to meet afterwards at 5pm by the trees.

I was impressed by the forcefulness of the argument that it was time for direct action. I went to the where the group were meeting along with Gina, a friend who I was with. Gina was the daughter of a school

Greenham Common Women's Peace Camp

friend of my mum's. Gina belonged to a family also heavily involved with CND and who had set up 'Teachers for Peace'. It was gratifying to think I'd finally be doing something more direct and meaningful. I had been on many demonstrations but things felt much more urgent now.

We were told that the action was to be the next day; we were to meet at 7am at the Jubilee Gardens, opposite the Houses of Parliament. It meant missing the coach back to York that night but I reassured myself that it was only for one night and I could stay with Gina. The action was planned to highlight the levels of financial investment in the arms industry and to demonstrate against Reagan's visit.

Some women were going to hand out leaflets during the action, some would be legal observers and others were going to lie down on the road 'acting dead' to represent the likely death from a nuclear incident. This was quite something. Gina and I exchanged glances. She was up for this and so was I. We both wanted to be the ones lying in the road rather than have to deal with commuters. Each group would have a leader, and we'd follow them. We wouldn't know where we were going or which tube station until the very last minute. This was a tactic to avoid giving advance information to any police informer who could be present.

The next morning, after our meeting at Jubilee Gardens, we all headed off to the underground in the rush hour. I nervously got out of the underground station and saw that some women were already on the road. I ran over and joined them. We weren't planning to do it for more than 15 minutes.

Some motorists got angry and frustrated with not being able to get past, though no one was hurt. Fortunately, there were only a few arrests. I should have gone home, back to York then after that but there was talk of another action and I found being with the energetic and determined women very energising and addictive so I stayed in London longer. The planned action was to 'keen' whilst walking past the Houses of Commons. This 'keening' was a loud wailing noise' and quite an unsettling eerie sound, meant to demonstrate women's mourning of the destructiveness of war. I was told that traditionally women did this

A New Man

at funerals and we were attempting to replicate this type of expression.

There were about fifteen of us. We wore black clothes and we started keening as we crossed Westminster Bridge. Suddenly a police van drew up alongside and group of policemen cornered us, in a few seconds we were surrounded by them. Then we were bundled into the van with a policeman on each side of us. No one was cautioned we were just pushed into the van. We didn't have banners, we weren't even shouting out slogans, just making loud wailing noises. Maybe they were just freaked out by the sound, I don't know. I was very disappointed to be arrested just for this.

This was the first time I had ever been arrested and it wasn't even for anything substantial. I was taken to Bow Street Police Station, put in a police cell and then let out a few hours later but I had been charged. The police were relatively civil to me but I couldn't help thinking that charging us with an offence was an overreaction. I was charged with 'causing an obstruction to the highway' and informed that I would have to attend court. We had meetings planned later that week to work out what we would do. I took the opportunity to visit the few lesbian nightclubs in London whilst I had to wait for the meeting before returning to Yorkshire.

A court notice in the post was sent to me, I had to appear in a juvenile court in London. When the day arrived, I caught a train down to London. After finding the relevant room in the juvenile court house in Marylebone, I walked straight in. I had to be there for 10am and I was only just on time.

However, the reception I got was unexpected. A court official said in a concerned voice, 'Why have you come here on your own? Where are your parents?' Another woman asked, 'Don't you have a social worker?'

None of this made any sense to me. Why would my parents be with me? What social worker? I replied, 'I've come on my own from York, I don't know what you mean.'

I wasn't tried at the time. They said that they would be in contact. Eventually the court case was changed so that I could be tried with my fellow campaigners and by that time my seventeenth birthday had passed. I was much happier about this. It also meant that Helena Kennedy, the formidable barrister, would be representing us.

When the trial took place two months later, however, she was unable to obtain a 'not guilty' verdict for us though and we were instead 'bound over to keep the peace' for six months, something we all found hugely ironic. There were no fines to pay and I was informed that this 'breach of the peace' charge was only a civil offence, not criminal, so I wouldn't have a criminal record, though I had to stay out of trouble for six months, otherwise I would be sent straight to prison. I then returned to sixth form for a few more weeks before the end of the summer term.

One hot day in July during the summer holiday, I finally went to Greenham Common Women's Peace camp to see what it was like. I had met Toni and her girlfriend in the Carved Red Lion, a tiny lesbian club in a basement in Islington, London and the three of us went down together.

When we got off the coach at Newbury we didn't have a clue where to go, but eventually worked out that we had to walk quite a bit to get to the camp. When we finally arrived, about an hour later we saw there were some caravans and a few women talking and drinking tea. We felt uncomfortable at first as it was like invading someone's living room, but then gradually we started to talk to the women there and we did what many people did on first visiting the camp – we walked all around the nine-mile perimeter fence of the former second world war air base to take it all in and to see what America planned to be a nuclear missile base.

Overall the camp itself was very pleasant and relaxed, like a summer holiday camp, even. Some women gave massages, we read books, did lots of talking, went on walks, we relaxed. In the evening, often some of us would go to a local pub and play pool. Cooking was an issue for me as I still didn't want to have anything to do with it, but now of course this was different as there weren't any men around to serve. I was teased about it and I had to learn how to cut vegetables and we ate wholesome and healthy food.

A New Man

At the camp, there was a stand pipe for water provision. This was a legal requirement; the local council was obligated to provide the women with water. There was also a private camping toilet complete with tent. Mostly the camp survived on donations of food and money and what individual women could contribute. After a week, we went back to London but Toni and I especially, felt drawn to Greenham and we visited again.

Toni made a steam room, called a 'Sweat Lodge', which was popular. This was a tent-like structure with big stones that had been heated up and then had water poured on them to produce steam. I didn't go myself as being naked did not appeal. Even surrounded by women who were very accepting of everyone still did not make me feel comfortable in my body.

Learning not to offend the women at Greenham proved to be a challenge. Once I was walking through a path and kicked aside some bracken, I was rebuked for this for not respecting nature. In the evening, for entertainment, sometimes someone would play the guitar. I did enjoy the singing but once I casually said that we should 'Bring on the dancing girls!' And I was told off. I think this was just a remnant of watching so many Broadway films on Sundays with my mum. I bought a bar of chocolate in Newbury and the woman I was with flew into a rage because of the brand of the chocolate and their alleged complicity in animal torture.

My mum remarked that with just women together it would be intense as hell which I disagreed with at the time but now I think she had a point. The discussions would go on for hours and were exhausting. Nevertheless, at the same time, being in a women-only environment was also empowering and there were opportunities to become more involved in the heart of things and gain confidence.

I became confused about my identity in terms of class. Middle class women due to being more confident generally tended to speak to the media. I found it quite sad that this was interpreted by many that all the women at Greenham Common were middle class. I had a mother with an upper-class Colombian background but without the security

Greenham Common Women's Peace Camp

of a family, and who had worked as a cleaner and chamber maid as well as teacher; my dad had a working-class background. Eventually I just reasoned that the combined worlds made me lower middle class.

I found the identity politics of the 1980s challenging. An example of this was when I visited a friend and casually picked up a newsletter on the kitchen table and asked if I could look at it, I was then asked if I considered myself 'Working Class' The newsletter was only to be read by working class lesbians it turned out and so not for me. I felt awkward, I had made a faux pax.

During the summer of 1982, I was enjoying my time at Greenham Common and was excited by the dynamism of the women at the camp even though there were only a few actions during the summer. I had long stopped thinking of myself as male. I just thought that I had internalised society's idea of what was male and that I could be strong and un-feminine and still be female.

I had become involved briefly in a three-way relationship with Toni and her girlfriend but it had ended fairly quickly. They had a strong bond and I was inexperienced and just a visitor in their world. I longed for a meaningful relationship of my own. There were many formidable women at Greenham for whom I had a lot of admiration. I longed for a relationship but nothing serious materialised.

For Hiroshima day on August 6th, it was agreed that we should do something special. It was decided to commemorate the day by creating a representation of the number of people who died in the first instance on 6th August 1945. And we would do this by gathering 100,000 stones – each a unique representation of a human life that had ended on that day – and place them on the war memorial in Newbury at the exact time the first nuclear bomb had dropped on the unsuspecting people going about their business.

It took longer than we thought it would to count all these stones. By the evening of August 5th, we still didn't have enough stones so we continued through the night using car headlights so that we could carry on collecting. In the morning, we drove off in cars taking the sacks of stones to Newbury and placed them carefully on the war memorial

A New Man

steps. We were dressed in black as we walked around the memorial in silence.

Unfortunately, this commemoration was not at all well received by some local people, who became very angry with us. One local youth kicked the stones off swearing at us and some women were arrested by the police and later charged with 'dropping litter'. The following day the local newspaper reported that we had desecrated the memorial and insulted the dead who had fought against the Japanese.

It felt upsetting to be so misunderstood. We had been earnest and worked hard in wanting to commemorate the deaths of all those thousands of people in one instant of the nuclear explosion. We felt the individual stones with their different colours, sizes and shapes were perfect in their representations of human life. Some passers-by, when asked, did place a stone on the memorial steps so that was some compensation.

As the summer was coming to an end, I had to decide what to do. I was only intending to stay at Greenham Common for the summer as I was supposed to go back to York and finish my A-levels. I returned to York and collected my re-take results but they were abysmal. I disappointed the General Studies teacher so much by only getting a D grade that he actually said, 'I'm going to kick your fanny!' when he saw me in the school corridor which was horrible and just made me want to return to Greenham Common immediately. It was nonetheless very disappointing and a knock to my self-esteem to have done that badly. All in all, I only obtained three O-levels above C grade, whereas both Marta and Colin had obtained nine each in their day. Some people in my class had parents that paid for re-marking when they had got Ds' and they all got moved up to the C grades, which I thought was unfair.

Toni went back to London but I wanted to stay at Greenham. I found the camaraderie exciting and compelling. I felt a growing belief in our collective power and felt empowered being part of such a fearless ground-breaking movement.

I wondered if I could continue with studying at the college in Newbury which was close to the camp. I started looking into this possibility and after some form filling and a couple of interviews I entered the further education college in Newbury in September to continue with my French A level and I started studying Politics instead of Sociology. This seemed the best of both worlds and the bonus was that I wouldn't have any more money problems as I would not have to pay any rent. It also met with Marta's approval as she wanted me to continue studying.

The plan was to go to college using the camp bicycle and then study at night in the caravans and this started well. I made friends with local students, I enjoyed the studying too. But after the summer, the camp changed. It got colder and there were fewer women around. Then the eviction took place, which put an end to the studying. It was early in the morning on 29th September when the police came and read out the legal notices and then the crane operators and lorry drivers set to work. Not only did the caravans get hoisted away but the council also dumped huge boulders and rubble onto the large grass verges of the road with the aim of preventing us from returning and pitching up tents.

After they had gone, the scene was depressing, with practically nothing of the camp left, even the toilet tent had been taken. It was raining and cold. What were we going to do? On the day of the eviction there were only eleven women at the camp. A woman who lived locally came to help and took some women to her house to dry out. Some blankets and cooking equipment had also been saved. The determination of many of the women there was infectious, but there was no question that the camp would close.

That night some women still managed to sleep over at the camp that night in a hidden bender (a dome-shaped structure of bendy wood and plastic covering). Many of us became quite good at making these temporary structures. I then made one with some help too and I tried to do my homework in the candlelight.

Life at the camp became tough for me. The weather turned, it was extremely cold and wet and it was a struggle to fulfil ordinary daily needs. Privacy was difficult for washing and going to the toilet as now the camp toilet tent had been evicted. Pits were dug for hygiene reasons.

A New Man

We tried to hold meetings in the continual rain and to keep information and leaflets dry but it was nigh-on impossible. For hours, we sat huddled round the fire drinking hot drinks holding umbrellas and having to put up with the smoke that changed direction continually.

The women who remained were a mixture of ages, from about 17 years old (me and one other) to about 50 years old. We weren't all lesbians, and came from a variety of backgrounds, one was German too but we were all resolutely determined to try and stop the 'tactical' nuclear weapons being brought to Greenham Common.

Perversely the conditions made it even harder to leave. We wanted to support each other and I think we also would've felt guilty by leaving others behind so we stuck it out. This eviction, as far as the authorities were concerned, was meant to be the final eviction and we noticed the harassment by police went up to another level, following us around and not leaving us alone.

One morning, construction workers began to dig up the land outside the base. We discovered this was in order to lay more pipes to accommodate an increased number of US servicemen within the base. We tried to disrupt the work and about thirteen of us laid down on the ground where they wanted to excavate. We thought we would be moved away and just cautioned but then one woman who spoke to the media often, Rebecca, was arrested. She went limp as we all did to practice a non-violent disobedient method of being arrested and then others, including me, were also arrested and we did the same. It wasn't considered a good look to walk willingly to the police van and at the same time we didn't want there to be any possibility of a charge of 'resisting arrest' too.

We were charged with 'breach of the peace' again. The court case was due to take place in November and I wondered whether I should agree to be 'bound over to keep the peace again' or go to prison as others had. I started to think that maybe I should do the latter. Apart from the obvious insult that we were supposedly 'breaching the peace' we also thought it would be the right statement to make.

There was a clear moral reason in my mind to opposing the coming of the new US nuclear missiles in England, so I wasn't afraid of prison. I was curious in fact: I wanted to see for myself first hand exactly what prison was like. I wasn't scared as I thought I'd be with the other women I'd been arrested with who were also contemplating refusing to be bound over and I wouldn't be inside for long either. I talked to other women who'd been inside. The thought of it being a problem for my future career or it being a shameful thing didn't enter my head.

The date for the trial was set for 17th November 1982 in Newbury Magistrates court. We decided to defend ourselves; this meant that each of us had our own opportunity to say in public and on the record, why we had taken the action and to try and influence the outcome. When it was my turn, although I was nervous I had written some notes to help me and I spoke about the massive financial investment in nuclear weapons that could and should be used instead for hospitals and schools. I said that I resented the fact that I had been arrested and charged with causing a breach of the peace whereas in fact I had been trying to promote peace.

Katrina, a very self-assured woman, who had been involved with Greenham since its inception, said to the magistrates that they were supporting nuclear weapons and silencing women's voices of warnings of death.

The judges didn't accept our defence and asked us to accept to be bound over to keep the peace but most of us decided that we would not agree to their definitions of 'keeping the peace' and we didn't agree so we were, as we predicted, sent down. The standard length of time was fourteen days for not agreeing to be bound over, so we knew beforehand it was going to be two weeks. Some women were taken to a prison in Kent and me and the remaining eleven were taken to a so called 'open' women's prison in Staffordshire, called 'Drake Hall'. I wondered what I'd let myself in for.

8

Imprisonment

It seemed a strong gesture walking out of court with our fists high in defiance, but it was with trepidation that I walked downstairs to the cells. I could hear people shouting 'shame' to the magistrates as I walked down. The seriousness of the situation began to sink in and I felt uneasy. I had been advised to bring a bag of clothes and wash things so I had them with me. There then followed a lot of form filling at the police station before they made the prison arrangements.

I had already said to my politics lecturer at the Newbury College that I may go to prison. Initially she was lost for words, then she'd replied as long as it wasn't for a long time it wouldn't be a problem. I fully intended to try and return to college even without the caravans to do my homework in but things became more chaotic from this time in prison onwards and so I didn't return to Newbury College.

Hours passed in the police cells until finally at 7pm, we were put in a van with each of us locked in small tight cubicle with a small ledge to sit on with no seat belts. After an arduous journey up the M5 in the small cubicle, occasionally being thrown against the steel wall, we finally arrived at the prison. I peered out of the tiny window, trying to see what it looked like. I could only make out flat buildings, it didn't look like a prison, there weren't any big walls, there was no sign of barbed wire, it looked more like a hospital, if anything. What an awful place Drake Hall prison turned out to be though. It was like a cross between a psychiatric institution and a boarding school for the less financially advantaged.

After arriving, we first had to be stripped and silly petty things were removed from us, anything that would signify status such as watches for example weren't allowed and the paper branding in my tobacco pouch was even removed because it wasn't a standard UK brand. I

Imprisonment

asked why and was told I wasn't allowed to stand out, to be special.

Three hours of documentation later and I was presented in front of the prison doctor. I was asked if I'd ever attempted suicide and he checked my arms for needle marks, and felt me to see if I was pregnant. We had checked up on our rights beforehand so I knew that I could refuse to be photographed and refused to have my finger prints taken. Finally, at 1am, after all the documentation and checking had been completed, we were taken to the bedrooms. A woman was asleep in the other bed in my allocated room, so I quietly undressed and slipped into my bed. I lay awake for a while wondering what the next day would be like before falling into a deep sleep.

At 6.30 am I was woken up by a shrill voice of an officer calling out 'Morning girls! Time to get up' I got up and left the room sharpish, and walked towards the wash rooms. I began brushing my teeth with the toothpaste powder I'd been given, but I had to spit it out, it was so repulsive. The other women prisoners were walking about in prison dressing gowns and nighties and were queuing up for the showers. They ignored me completely.

I met some other Greenham women, some had been put in rooms together, I wish I had. I finished washing and returned to the room. On the door to the room, I saw the label: C. Kiss D16247 on the door - my prison number. The other woman in my room didn't say anything to me other than I'd better neaten my side of the room otherwise we'd both be kept in.

Because it was an open prison, we were never locked up, instead you had your own key to the room (which you shared with the other prisoner) and then when evening came you had to give the key to the officer on duty. At least with locks in a closed prison you are left alone and have some basic privacy. At this prison, every half an hour during the night, an officer would come by and shine a torch on to your face to make sure you weren't up to any mischief.

At 7am I walked across the grounds with other Greenham women to the canteen clutching my plastic cup and knife and fork.

At the canteen entrance, I had to provide my prison number to be

63

A New Man

marked off a list, before being told to sit at a table where there was a place. Women were sitting around chatting, smoking, knitting and listening to their radios. I met two middle aged white women on my table, they were very friendly and interested to hear about Greenham common. They behaved as if they weren't bothered by prison life much at all, in fact they said that they regularly did 'insurance jobs' and tried to arrange it so that they were in prison during the winter. I wasn't sure if they were joking or not but they were clearly confident, unlike most of the women in the prison.

The breakfast food was awful. I had half a slice of burnt toast and a bit of the watery porridge. Sugar was only given out on Fridays, I learnt, the woman next to me generously gave me a bit of hers for my tea. I wondered how the vegetarians and vegans in our Greenham group would cope with the poor quality of food and not being able to eat half of it.

All the prisoners were demeaningly referred to as 'girls'. The women in the prison also acted like young girls too, some appeared to look up to the prison officers as if they were their guardians and many even called them 'Miss'.

The overwhelming majority of the women in the prison were unsurprisingly very unhappy to be there, especially those missing their children. The majority were inside due to poverty. One woman told me she was there because she hadn't been able to pay her television licence, others were inside for shoplifting.

In prison, little things take on bigger importance and something as ordinary as proper toothpaste is a luxury. The old-fashioned tooth cleaning powder provided tasted of baking soda, and the toilet paper was stiff and scratched. In order to obtain the coveted proper toothpaste and decent toilet paper, you'd have to save up from your weekly wages and one week's wage was not enough to buy the smallest packet of tobacco and a roll of toilet paper so you had to make a hard choice. Prisoners eked out items for as long as possible, for example they'd split matches with a pin so that one match could be split into four or more matches.

Imprisonment

The work we were given was purse assembly and we had to stitch them together. The hours were 8am to 4pm. Some work was available in the gardens, kitchens or laundry for longer-term inmates. Work in prison was a strange business, I deduced. On the one hand, it made sense to be doing something to prevent total boredom. On the other hand, the work was basically boring factory work and the pay tokenistic. We wondered about the companies who benefitted from this captive cheap labour arrangement. It also seemed that a lot of the functioning of the prison was entirely facilitated by the inmates.

In the evening, we had a two hour 'association time' slot on the wing where the available activity was watching TV. At 9pm everyone had to go to bed and all the lights were switched off.

That night after my first day in prison, I lay in bed thinking about how fasts things had developed since first meeting some Greenham Women after the CND demonstration only a few months earlier. I thought of Marta, and hoped she wasn't worried. I was fine though. I felt empowered being in a group of women.

After only being there a few days, we made the decision after a quick meeting in the canteen to refuse to work. All of us were then locked up, two per cell in the punishment block called, 'Allen House'. As there were only six cells in total, we filled the block and thereby prevented anyone else being sent there to be punished, which was gratifying.

We were locked up for 24 hours apart from half an hour twice per day when we could exercise. We did some karate exercises during these, but in the cells, I found it excruciatingly boring and time went so slowly.

For maximum discomfort, mattresses and blankets and pillows were removed from 6:45am to 5pm. Leaving only a metal bed frame. There was nothing to read, nothing to write with. At least I wasn't alone and my cellmate, Kath was good company and we talked and talked and laughed and talked until we could talk no more. Kath was from Brighton, she didn't live at the camp, but would just visit from time to time. She was only a bit older than me and we had a similar outlook on life.

When I was in the block I was thrilled to receive an enormous bou-

A New Man

quet of flowers, it had been sent from Camden Council Trades Council. I assume they chose my name at random but it cheered me up no end. I used to think flowers were silly and overly feminine prior to receiving these. My attitude changed completely.

Eventually after five days, me and Kath, decided a few days in the punishment block was more than enough and returned to work as we felt we were starting to lose our sanity. We were just too bored. This had been only a few days. It made me marvel as to how people who are locked up for months and years with no contact with other people mentally and emotionally survive. I suspected they never properly recover.

I put in a governor's application to move in to the same room as Kath and amazingly, I was given permission. I arranged all the cards that we had received from friends and well-wishers on top of the wardrobe and put the flowers in the vase and looked forward to the next day where there would be more to do than just lie on a metal bed frame.

Although we had agreed to do the work, we only manged to stitch two purses and then we were allowed to go to the gym, where we played basketball. We bought coffee and sugar. We both agreed we had done the right thing coming out of Allen House.

But the next morning early at 6 am, without warning we were woken up and instructed to get our stuff. We were being moved.

There had been a vigil outside the main entrance to the prison for us and we hoped we'd be able to alert the people outside on the vigil as we drove past, that all the Greenham women in Drake Hall were being moved out but we were taken out the back entrance.

We had a police escort to the front and rear of us which was bizarre, and we couldn't understand why that was necessary as we were hardly dangerous. We were transported in two ordinary mini-coaches rather than the horrible claustrophobic small-cage prison vans with the cubicles. We asked where we were being sent to and all we could get out of the officers was that we were 'going south'. It was disconcerting not knowing where. Then the coaches separated. Our coach proceeded to stop at other institutions. We were all being split up into smaller groups

Imprisonment

across many different prisons. Then finally my coach with just four of us left inside, Katrina, Clare and Helen and I arrived at Holloway Women's Prison in North London. Our solicitors had to be informed where we had been taken and so we knew word would get out soon. I suspected the plan to treat us softly had not worked as we had rebelled and now we were going to get harsher treatment in a closed prison.

Holloway was different. I was put in a cell on my own on the borstal wing for young offenders, because I was seventeen. I was interviewed by a large older Scottish ex-RAF woman who was intimidating. She made it quite clear to me that she didn't consider me to be any different from anyone else at prison and that I needed to buck my ideas up. I didn't know what to say to her. I didn't consider myself a wayward teenager, I saw myself as more of a political prisoner. I looked at her intently. I was determined not to be intimidated by here and I felt hostile. She growled at me and said, 'You can't outstare me'.

The rest of the sentence was depressing. I talked to the old woman in the cell next to me through the slatted windows, but she was almost incoherent. She told me she was there because she'd stolen ten teddy bears. She seemed completely harmless. At night, it was difficult sleeping because of the screaming and banging that went on all through the night. Half an hour in the morning and again in the afternoon, we would have exercise which consisted of walking round in a circle in a yard. I thought that had died out in the nineteenth century.

Apart from eating in the dining room of the wing, with other women on the wing and the two half-hour exercise sessions each day, I had to spend the rest of the time alone in my cell. There was nothing to do at all. Some of the women on the wing looked tough but everyone was drugged up and zombified. I kept myself to myself.

It was a peculiar thing, I thought, that you never were ever able to finish your meal. You'd always be about three quarters of the way through and then you'd be told to go back to your room and have to take your plate with you back into your cell to finish. It seemed deliberate, perhaps so that time with others and restlessness was kept to a minimum. The food was extremely poor and very stodgy with no fresh

A New Man

fruit or vegetables.

Despite the screws attempting to treat us as ordinary prisoners, my experience was much easier being with other Greenham women than for someone coming in on their own for the first time. I imagine it would be frightening.

However, after only four nights in a cell on my own, Holloway had quite an effect on me. I had developed a protective attitude to the cell and I didn't want anyone to come in. I realised that I felt slightly institutionalised even by my ridiculously short time in prison.

When it was time to leave on Tuesday morning, there was a bang on the door. For a few moments, I didn't want to leave my precious space, my own cell. Then there was all the bureaucracy again. I was weighed and forms were filled out. 'You weigh more now than when you came in prison!' I was told as if that was a good thing but it wasn't much of a revelation given the stodgy nature of the food and the fact I had been locked up for most of the sentence.

There was a big crowd waiting to welcome just the four of us. That was nice but it was also a bit overwhelming, we didn't feel like heroines. The press was there and we were expected to give interviews immediately. We were given champagne, lager and flowers. Katrina, Clare, Helen and I had our photos taken by some journalists. Our release was featured in The Guardian as well as the Tribune and the Morning Star. Islington council even offered us a champagne reception but we refused because we didn't want to be seen as heroines, as 'stars.' We said we'd continue the campaign, the fight against the cruise missiles and we returned to Greenham later that day by train, courtesy of HM Prison Holloway as prison authorities allowed for a paid rail ticket 'home' on release.

When we got back to Greenham, it was almost as if we'd never been away. There had been many of us released from prison that day and it was almost a non-event coming back to the camp but it was good of course to see everyone again. The preparations for the big action due to take place were well under way and I became completely absorbed in that. We were released on November 30th and the surround the base

Imprisonment

action was due to take place on December 12th, 1982. The advertising and promotion of this event was purely by word of mouth and chain letters. In the days before email, Twitter and Facebook, the success of the action surpassed our expectations.

Some women saw the action as 'surrounding the base' to demonstrate the massive opposition to the base, others with a more spiritual bent, saw the action as 'embracing the base,' an action to change the 'energy of the base' with the positive life energy of all the women believing in life of the planet, of mother earth. I preferred the former viewpoint; I had a lot of difficulty in relating to the spirituality dimension that many women at the camp promoted.

I was also troubled by what I saw as the oversimplification of the relationship of masculinity to violence and war at Greenham. To my mind this was more related to positional power rather than the belief that men themselves were inherently violent. I wasn't the only one who found this difficult; a friend who visited disliked the notion that women were naturally peaceful and passive, it made her very angry and she even felt that the doctrine of the camp was anti-feminist.

The discussions and beliefs centred a lot on men being the problem and being surrounded by this mentality every day affected me and I tended to agree with much of this viewpoint. Men would visit and insist that they were peaceful and they wanted the right to oppose the missiles too. It must have been incredibly frustrating for them. It was however, reiterated continually that there were other sites that the missiles were due to be installed at and that Molesworth Peace Camp was a mixed peace camp and men could go there.

On a practical level, it did make some sense not to have men on actions, as the police would undoubtedly have been more violent if men had been involved. Finally, the symbolism of women who are rarely instigators and perpetuators of war saying 'no to life-threatening nuclear weapons was very powerful.

Not many people are aware that the camp at Greenham started off with some men as well, (it started with 36 women and four men) but it was decided about seven months later that the camp would function

A New Man

better if it became exclusively female. I heard that an example of the difficulties prior to this, was that journalists, on arrival at the camp, would immediately speak to men at the camp as if they were in charge.

Having been prevented from having caravans or proper structures by the authorities, the main problems at hand were coping with the weather. We hung a line between two trees, draped plastic over it and placed pallets underneath and this became a makeshift long tent that I along with others then slept in.

The big day arrived, the day of the major action; the surrounding of the base on December 12th. I had a walkie-talkie, along with about ten other women around the base. The plan was that once the base was completely encircled we would let everyone know.

Hundreds of coach loads arrived full of women from all over the country. It was technically an illegal demonstration as it had not been given official permission. There were difficulties in obtaining marquees initially and toilet tents once the hire companies knew what the event was, which was a problem because we could have really done with many more of both because far more women than expected arrived, we had hoped for 10,000 as we had calculated that would be enough to surround the base if women held out their arms fully stretched. It's well documented now that more than three times that number of women attended. Most who attended put items on the fence that meant something to them. A photo of their child, for example. Some wove images with wool. It was an incredible success, an original way of demonstrating. Poignant photos of these items were printed in the papers.

The next day was a Monday, and blockades were planned at all the entrances to the base to prevent it being operational. Again, very successful, though only two to three thousand of the original thirty thousand stayed. It would have been more successful if more had been able to stay. The police, though were rougher than they had ever been when removing women from the blockades of the entrances to the base. There weren't the local police and so they hadn't got used to the methods of protesting at Greenham.

I wondered what would have happened if there had been men in

Imprisonment

the protest. Would the men have retaliated? Because the women didn't. Would the police have been more violent with men present in the protest? I thought that it was highly likely. Although I suspect that the police were able to get around this, psychologically, by seeing us as brutish lesbians. I was very upset to see a photo of a friend crying out in pain, after a policeman had kicked her in the back, being presented as a face of anger in a tabloid newspaper. It looked as if they had manipulated the picture to present a false image of us being aggressive.

Press attention increased significantly after the success of the action, and it was extremely intrusive. Rather than focussing on the nuclear weapons and the actions against the base, the journalists wrote about the things like the difficulties of trying to make a cup of tea in the rain and the lesbians at the camp. They also wanted us to perform for them, and repeat getting out of the tent for example to get the best picture. This was not appealing at all. We wanted to focus on the base not on the difficulties of living outside it.

I suppose it was inevitable that the press would focus on the trivial and sensational but this was problematic. We didn't have structure, given that we considered structure patriarchal and restrictive, so the notion of a PR unit or strategy to improve our media image was never even contemplated. Individuals just took it upon themselves to do the best they could. A female journalist from 'The Daily Mail' stayed on the camp without revealing who she was and wrote the most disparagingly offensive article and even made a lot of stuff up.

On top of having to deal with intrusive journalists, after the success of the 'surround the base' action we were inundated with hundreds of visitors and substantial amounts of presents. A good thing really, but it became exhausting answering the same questions repeatedly, especially the dreaded 'Where do you get your water from?'

In addition to the presents, as Christmas was fast approaching, we received Christmas cakes, hundreds of mince pies, turkeys even and tons and tons of alcohol, far too much to drink.

Because of the cold and wet weather with difficult living conditions many of us began drinking a bit too much of the readily available booze. Obviously, the plethora of drink was not a good development and without wishing to cause offence to visitors we realised we had to start refusing the alcohol. So, we started accepting a bottle from visitors and offering a different one in return and explaining that we just had too much. We also distributed boxes of food and Christmas goodies to local homes and shelters; we even gave some items to people going inside the base. There was also too much food to eat and inevitably without airtight containers we got visited by rats, which was really horrible. I was convinced that rats ran under the pallets we were sleeping on and I dreamt that one nibbled some crumbs from my lips.

Naturally the press had a field day and called us 'the dirty women of Greenham Common' but if the caravans hadn't been evicted and if we had been allowed to put up tents then things could have been much cleaner and more organised.

Still, there was something that we tried to keep our focus on and this was a planned action to get to the location inside the base where the missiles would be housed: the cruise missile silos which were huge concrete structures. There was a core group of us who were keen to carry this out. The plan was to highlight the fact that 1983 was a crucial pivotal year in the arms race and that to prevent further international destabilisation, the cruise missiles due to arrive at Greenham Common USAF had to be stopped.

Reaching the silos would mean breaching the fence. It was considered unacceptable to cut the fence at this stage, as this was deemed violent and it would also be classed as criminal damage, a criminal offence. It was challenging making progress with decisions on the action because every day more women arrived and wanted to be involved. At one point, we were having three meetings per day to discuss the action. Then someone had the idea of using ladders and carpets to go over the barbed wire at the top of the perimeter fence to circumvent the issue of cutting the fence. This was agreed upon as a solution, so some women drove off to another local town and bought about twelve ladders. They said they were a women's theatre group and needed some light aluminium ladders for a play.

Imprisonment

At four am, on the day of the action, New Year's Day of 1983 I was in the back of a big van being driven along the country lanes with a scalpel cutting the protective plastic away from the ladders. This was dangerous with the van lurching from side to side as we drove. I couldn't help laughing slightly hysterically. This should have been done before we set off in the van.

We had to carry the ladders into the bushes near to the fence without alerting the US military police who were guarding the silos. The media had been notified in advance and there were many of them there waiting with us with their cameras and lights in the bushes for us to climb over.

There was a worry that the American soldiers could freak out and shoot us, so it was decided that we had to do the invasion just as dawn was breaking so that we could be seen. Michael Heseltine, the Defence minister had admitted only days before in the House of Commons that the American soldiers were legally able to fire at any intruders, causing an outcry by the British public but then the missiles hadn't arrived yet and it was thought extremely unlikely.

Placing the ladder against the fence, throwing a piece of carpet over the barbed wire then lifting a second ladder to drop the other side of the fence worked well. Most of us got over the fence quickly and then we ran as fast as we could through a gap in the many fences (for the vehicles) until we got to the foot of the silos. There we had to scramble up the side of the massive concrete silos. I was exhilarated, we all were. At the top, we spontaneously held hands then walked round in a circle, slowly speeding up until we were effectively dancing. Not everyone made it to the top but forty-four of us did. We were photographed on top of the silos at dawn and the photo became iconic. The headline of one newspaper was 'Greenham Women go over the top' which was a quite amusing reference to the soldiers of the First World War.

It goes without saying we were all arrested but we were relieved to be only charged with breach of the peace again rather than under the Official Secrets Act which had a potential 14-year sentence. Following this we had a good couple of days in the Newbury police cells, we were

A New Man

getting to know the police well and it was even quite friendly between us. We had newspapers brought in, we were allowed to smoke in the cells and spend time out of the cells in a communal area within the police station and spirits were high. We were released with an expected court date in February.

A New Year's Eve party was arranged in a local community Hall by some of the women back at the camp to celebrate New Year and the success of the action.

Left: Marta with Jaime in Colombia in 1956
Above: Marta with Dad in Versailles
Below: Wedding in 1959

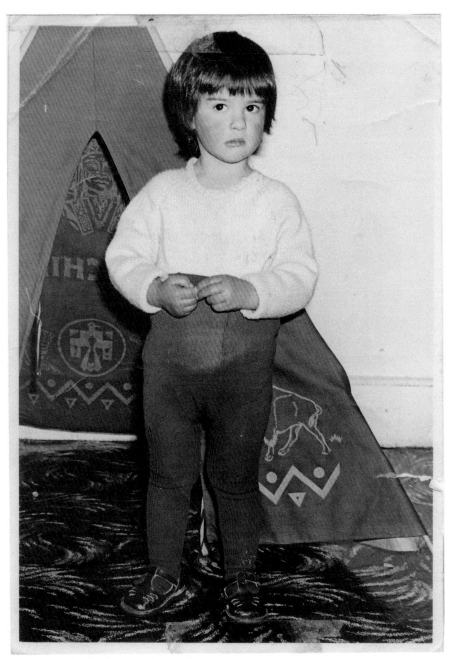

At nursery in Kilburn

Above: 'Little Fair Oak' in Devon
Below left: First wellington boots aged 5
Below right: Marta, Justina, me and the chickens

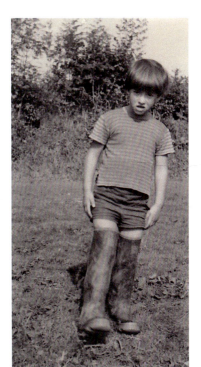

Above: Justina and me in the bath
Below: On Brighton beach aged 6

Right: With scruffy hair aged 9
Below: Caravan home in Yorkshire

 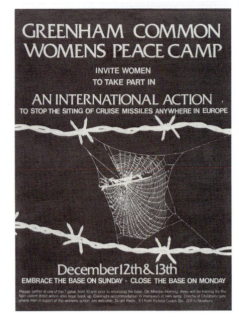

Above left: Eviction Day, 29th September 1982
Above right: Leaflet advertising the December action

Release from Holloway Prison aged 17
Photo by Andrew Wiard

As dawn broke on January 1st 1983, the year the nuclear missiles were due to arrive, we scaled the perimeter fence using aluminum ladders and scrambled up to the top of the missile silos - the hardened concrete structures built to house the missiles. When we reached the top, we were so exhilarated we spontaneously held hands and danced.
Photo by Raissa Page/Format Photographers Archive

Above: At Greenham Common, June 1983
Below: With Rebekah by Regent's Canal, Islington, Summer 1983

9

Escaping to Holloway Prison

Brenda, an older woman who I'd recently met at the camp, drove to the off-licence in her car to get some booze for the party. I went with her. She asked what I fancied and I chose a bottle of Drambuie which Brenda paid for. I was looking forward to the party; it was about time we had some fun. Brenda was in her mid-forties and wealthy compared to me, she'd lived abroad before returning to England and had only recently arrived at the camp. She called herself a witch. She believed that she had special spiritual powers. This was unnerving to me and I didn't have the slightest interest in her beliefs or activities. Of course, I was aware that there were women who used herbs for medicines who were accused of being witches in earlier centuries, but I didn't believe in special powers.

We walked into the village hall where the party was held. It was quite late in the evening and the scene in front of us was pretty wild with much merriment; dancing, drinking, laughing and kissing. It seemed as if a lot of tension was being released following the stress of the silos action. I got very drunk on the Drambuie, and when Brenda started kissing me, I went along with it but I moved away from her when I could and instead kissed another woman, Corrie, who was only a year older than me. To me all of this was harmless fun. Lots of women at the party were being flirtatious and were also kissing other women. One woman even said afterwards, that it was like an orgy.

Corrie was sleeping, as I was, under the plastic sheeting, so back at the camp after the party we just carried on kissing and making out. The next morning, Corrie had a couple of love bites visible on her neck from me. Brenda appeared in the afternoon and after seeing Corrie she came up to me and said, 'You've got violent tendencies, you have,' and she said it with a mischievous, ambiguous approving tone. I was confused; it seemed an over-interpretation to me but obviously, she was also jealous and I felt guilty for having led her on.

I was still inexperienced sexually and I yearned to be better at sex. So, coupled with feeling guilty and wanting to avoid any emotional drama was my eagerness to become a proficient lover and I slept with her a few days later. This was a big mistake. Brenda said that I was strong and powerful. She told me I was into S&M too. Being told I was powerful made me feel good, though I didn't feel especially powerful and I really wasn't sure about her assertion about me being interested in S&M.

However, any personal power I had with Brenda was an illusion and this was abundantly clear from the moment we had sex. She took complete control and stated that I had to be completely quiet, no talking or moaning or any verbal expressions of enjoyment at all was allowed. She also demanded that my eyes were fully open at all times. Brenda totally flattened me.

She took me to her house. I was exhausted and tired from living at Greenham and admittedly it was a break to be taken away to a warm comfortable house. We had a nice hot bath. Brenda made it clear that we would be having sex afterwards. I didn't object. She worked out that I'd not had an orgasm before and seemed to relish in this. After what seemed like ages she announced she'd given me an orgasm. I could barely tell. I felt tense and didn't feel good at all. I felt like I was her project. Despite having girl-friends at the age of seven, I was a late developer sexually probably because I wasn't comfortable with having a female body. I knew the theory and had read about lesbian sex, it was just I had little desire for anyone to do anything to me.

I was nervous of upsetting her. She was very controlling. When we were driving, she suddenly started screaming. Alarmed I asked, 'What's the matter?'

'I just felt the need to scream, and so I shall scream when I want,' she said.

She also shaved off all her hair, she said this was a reminder to herself to stop drinking. I thought her behaviour was peculiar and it disturbed me.

Escaping to Holloway Prison

Back at the camp, one night to escape the continual rain, I went with a group of women to a nearby supporter's house, for some respite, where some women were sleeping over.

There wasn't much availability bed-wise and Brenda asked me to go into a single bed with her. I duly complied. I then misunderstood a sexual request of hers and I didn't do what she wanted, though I thought I had. She became very angry, I turned over on my side in despair, but this enraged her more. She started hammering me on my back with her fists and then she bit deep into my shoulders again and again. I was so shocked at her fury that I didn't get out of the bed. I just took the punishment and I just lay there crying and confused until she stopped.

It was years later when it dawned on me what I had done wrong and that she was in fact asking me to penetrate her deeply. I was simply inexperienced and on reflection I didn't desire this myself so didn't understand it on a basic level. At that time, in the early 1980s, the lesbian feminist viewpoint that everyone I knew seemed to agree with, was that in a relationship everything had to be completely equal. Anything remotely involving power in relationships was deemed akin to heterosexual sex. Lying on top of each other, and especially penetration, was frowned upon.

Andrea Dworkin a radical feminist writer of the time wrote: 'Intercourse is the pure, sterile, formal expression of men's contempt for women.'

This episode of misunderstanding with Brenda was misinterpreted that I was teasing her and then this impregnated into her mind the insidious idea that I was into sadomasochism, a rumour which appeared to spread at the camp. I became slightly paranoid.

I wore black, this was more of a hangover from my punk CRASS days, and there any similarity stopped with sadomasochism at least I had thought so. I started having niggling concerns as to whether I was actually into S&M from a masochistic point of view, which wasn't what Brenda meant, as she implied I was motivated by power and therefore, a sadist. I felt ambivalent about the soreness and welts on my back caused by Brenda's nails as I felt something close to enjoyment in the

A New Man

pain. I had a low opinion of myself but also when I leant against a chair and it hurt, it reminded me of my sexual activities, my masculine behaviour, of when I was on top. I was certain, however, that I didn't want to cause anyone else harm though and the notion of me having any power was laughable. I couldn't talk about any of these confusing thoughts about S&M to anyone at Greenham because I was sure I wouldn't get a sympathetic ear.

I went to visit Marta with Brenda who drove me there. Marta was polite but quietly unimpressed. We didn't stay long. When we got in the car to leave, Brenda turned to me and said, 'You and your mum have a very special bond, you could have a great sexual relationship'

I looked at her disgusted and said, 'You've got to be joking, how can you think such a thing!'

She persisted, 'If it wasn't against society's taboos, I believe you and your mother would have a great relationship as the two of you are so close.'

I didn't reply. I was lost for words.

After that visit, I had a break from Greenham and then went back to stay with Marta alone. I was exhausted from the very difficult conditions living at the camp and the emotional demands Brenda made on me. I came down with a severe cold and I had splitting headaches.

I wanted to run away from Brenda but I felt trapped. She had friends at Greenham, of course, and lived there some of the time. Since my home was at Greenham, everyone I knew apart from my family was there. I worried that Brenda was going around telling everyone that I was into sadomasochism. So, I tried to avoid being there.

Although I had commenced driving lessons at Newbury near to Greenham, I stopped the lessons so that I didn't have to remain at the camp. In any case, it was impossible concentrating during these lessons as the driving instructor couldn't stop talking about nuclear weapons throughout and that was distracting.

I then heard another woman was needed for a Greenham speaking trip in Norway, someone who would be appropriate to accompany Rebecca. My name was suggested and I jumped at the chance to leave

England, do something worthwhile and escape Brenda. At Greenham, we were often being asked to provide for speakers at various political events.

Rebecca was sensible and a confident speaker. I had a lot of respect for her so I was delighted to go to Oslo for a few days. Given who I was with I couldn't help but take a back seat and I didn't do a great deal of talking and Rebecca did most of it but I gave an interview for the Socialist Youth Paper there and with renewed confidence a few days later back in London, I gave a talk alone to a Girls School in Vauxhall.

The court case for the Silos action was coming up in mid-February and I had to attend meetings in Newbury or in London with the solicitors along with the other women charged to plan our defence. Many women were even hopeful that we could convince the judges to find us not guilty.

Shortly before the court case I became ill with a throat infection. I needed to see a doctor. I ended up relying on Brenda again as she took me to her own doctors. (I wasn't registered with any practice) and I was given a course of antibiotics.

At the court case I had much less energy to give a strong defence this time round but there were also many more of us this time, so that took some pressure off me. Expert witnesses came from all over the world, to give evidence as to why our actions superseded the worse crime of having nuclear weapons based a few miles from the court building we were in.

This time in court I was on autopilot. I thought it was very likely that we would be found guilty and sent down again. (Though I should point out that for future Greenham actions at Crown Courts some juries did acquit) but I thought that at least prison would allow me to escape from the suffocating relationship that I didn't have the strength to extract myself from.

Brenda did do something nice for me though, she bought me a radio for the time I'd be in prison. It would have been better if there had been time and space to talk things through with someone, then I would have concluded that I would've been better off out of the relationship and

A New Man

gained some support in managing to end it without fear but everyone was otherwise occupied and I hated asking for help or advice and I didn't want to be a burden. I hadn't known then that she tried it on with lots of young women at the camp.

With Corrie, she had slid one hand on her breast and her other hand into her knickers when Corrie was feeling a bit low and Brenda had got her alone. I was unaware that she had a thing about much younger women who she easily had power over. If only I'd been warned off her.

The Magistrates found us guilty with 'Breach of the Peace' as the charge again. Most of us refused to agree to be bound over to 'keep the peace' which automatically meant two weeks in prison. This time our destination was Holloway Prison from the start. After we had been strip-searched and processed, we arrived on the wing and a prisoner shouted at us,

'You bloody ban the bomb lot, I'm being moved out to Styal all because of you!'

Another woman explained to us that Styal was the worst prison to be sent to. We felt terrible. Because we were a large influx coming into Holloway at once, other prisoners were moved out. Styal prison in Cheshire was a prison with a worse reputation and the highest suicide rates in the UK for a women's prison but there wasn't anything we could do about it.

We felt that the screws were trying to divide us and set the current prisoners up against us so that we didn't have an easy time. The tactic largely failed because we were very sorry, others could see it wasn't our fault and we also began campaigns for all the prisoners for many things including better food.

I was put on a wing with seven other Greenham women. We were in the so-called cushy part of the prison, termed the 'therapy' wing but the only tangible benefits were tablecloths and flowers on the tables in the dining room.

I had to share my cell with one other Greenham woman, Eve. At least this time in Holloway I felt less isolated as there were thirty-eight of us in total who had refused to accept the binding order and consequently gone to prison. It seemed the authorities had given up on sending us to 'open prisons' and most of us were in closed prisons like Holloway.

Eve was a quiet woman, who wasn't living at the camp full-time so I didn't know her. She read a lot and kept herself to herself. We weren't similar at all, so we didn't talk much.

Sharing a confined space was awkward, and having to share a toilet with someone who was practically a stranger wasn't easy. There was no door to the toilet in the cell. I was envious of some of the other women who had been put in dormitory cells with about 6 to 8 beds. I imagined they were having much more fun.

I had been in prison for only two days when an excruciating pain developed in-between my legs. I didn't tell Eve because I was embarrassed at having such a personal problem. I had absolutely no idea what it was. The cells were excruciatingly hot, as prisoners we had no control over the temperature, or indeed anything. Each night I soaked my flannel with cold water and then placed it in between my legs, hoping Eve couldn't see, to soothe the pain and try and get some sleep. I didn't want to be seen as needy so I didn't ask for anyone's advice in the association time either. Consequently, this pain continued for the whole fortnight.

This time in prison I was better prepared or so I thought but when I arrived they took the radio from me even though I had ensured I had the right model stipulated which couldn't accept police radio waves. Their reason was that without earphones I could disrupt my cell mate. The previous time I'd been in a cell on my own and so I hadn't thought about this at all and I didn't remember seeing this instruction on the prison guidelines.

I started the process of trying to have earphones brought in for me. I got word out on one of my visits to have them sent in. Easy enough you would think, but the bureaucracy got in the way. To request anything in prison you have to fill out 'a Governor's application'. Then I was told that you could only do this on Tuesdays. What bureaucratic nonsense I thought, but I obliged and when the next Tuesday arrived, I duly

A New Man

completed the form and handed it in for the earphones so that I could have my radio in the cell.

With only a couple of days of the sentence left, a knock was heard on my cell door. The latch opened, and I expected to be given my radio finally and the earphones, but no, to my despair only the earphones were pushed through the hatch. I asked where the radio was, but I was told gleefully that I would need to fill out another governor's application the following Tuesday to get my radio as well by which time I would have left the prison. I was angry and then I was annoyed with myself for expecting anything reasonable, I should have known it was hopeless.

On Sunday evenings, we were given a treat as were on the 'therapy wing'; the treat was that the screws played the top ten hits for us from the radio in the wing loud enough so that we could all hear whilst we were locked up in the cells for the evening.

Pathetic as it might sound, we enjoyed this immensely.

I learnt about the 'muppet wing'. This was the term given to the wing for women who were seriously mentally ill. The sights of this wing were distressing; I looked out on one woman who just stood naked by her cell window staring out the whole day.

I didn't find out how ill you had to be to be sent there but the frustration and pent-up anger meant that sometimes women could be very strong and could rip radiators or sinks off the walls, which was one of the reasons 'calming' medication was regularly doled out. The Prison Reform Trust reports that 70% of women prisoners have two or more diagnosed mental health problems. It didn't seem right to me that mentally ill people should be locked in prison.

My mum was worried that I would be influenced by other prisoners and learns tricks on how to burgle and the like but there was little chance of that – the women in Holloway were in a very bad way psychologically and many went around in a drug induced daze. My experience of prison brought me to the conclusion that it was a very primitive, revengeful, mostly unnecessary and expensive way of dealing with society's problems by locking people away and ultimately is unsuccessful in preventing re-offending.

A solidarity peace camp had been set up directly outside Holloway prison for us inside. Toni and Gina were also at the camp outside the prison. They organised a rota for prison visits so every day we received a visit, unfortunately this meant my mum who'd driven up to London was unable to see me as my visit had already been taken.

On the night before our release some of the other inmates joked and sang a song 'I want to be Charlie's Girl' to the tune of 'I want to be Bobby's Girl'. I was quite touched at that. After leaving prison, I wrote to a couple of women inside but their sentences were short and after they were released we lost contact.

Our release day arrived. It would have been better if we could have walked out all together but they let us out one by one. When it was my turn, I had to walk the long stretch of path until I could get to the people waiting across the threshold and no one could come towards me to meet me as then they would have been entering prison property.

A large crowd awaited us – this time there were television cameras as well as newspaper journalists ready to interview us. There were Greenham women and many other supporters all cheering. I felt overwhelmed.

But standing in front of the crowd I saw the woman I had been desperate to avoid. Brenda was there with her arms outstretched, ready to grasp me back and she was screaming with delight. My heart sank. I felt like turning around and going back but I couldn't, I had no choice but to continue walking towards the crowd and towards Brenda. Once I reached the line I was enveloped by so many people congratulating me I was absorbed in that. I was handed some chocolate and lager and I was happy again for a moment.

After the interviews were done, we made our way to a party planned to celebrate our release. I tried to enjoy it and danced but Brenda was there, being demanding, one minute she was trying to dance with me, the next, crying her eyes out. Brenda wanted attention but I wished she would just leave me alone. I felt resentful and couldn't deal with her neediness.

A New Man

After the party, some of us went back to Toni's place nearby. I found a book on the shelves in the living room called, 'Our Bodies Ourselves' and looked up my symptoms as the pain between my legs hadn't gone away. Reading this, I determined that I almost certainly had thrush, brought on by taking the antibiotics for my throat infection and being in the obscenely hot environment of the prison cell. A suggested solution from the book was to bathe in water with vinegar added. I tried this straightaway and I recovered instantly. What absolute heaven. No more pain. I was extremely grateful to the book and pleased that I didn't have to try and see a doctor again.

Later that evening, in Toni's front room, when I was just spending some time alone, Brenda came in and knelt before me. It was unnerving. She looked up to me as if I was an all-powerful being sitting on a throne and wanted some attention. I felt repulsed and fed up with her framing me and manipulating me into an illusory powerful situation which was really one that was so imbalanced in her favour. I couldn't bear being in this false position any longer. I didn't believe I was the powerful one. She was. I didn't have the responsibility nor did I want it. I was disgusted and trapped. She wouldn't go away, she wouldn't leave me alone. I just wanted to be left alone, that's all I wanted. She placed her hands on my thighs and then I hit her, to push her out of my life once and for all. I had had enough. She hit me back and then we both laid into each other; we were an even match, pushing, grabbing and hitting each other.

Gina came into the room and pleaded with us to stop, she had no idea as to what was going on and even called out to us that we should stop and that we loved each other. That couldn't have been further from the truth. 'I don't love her!' I shouted with disdain. I felt I was fighting for my sanity.

Brenda, who was about 43, said quite openly that she preferred 'young blood'. Aged 17, I was completely under her thumb, but after the fight the relationship finally ended. She moved on to another young woman at Greenham shortly after me.

At the party, earlier, I heard some women talking and saying that

Escaping to Holloway Prison

they were planning on going to Comiso in Sicily. This was where the US military also planned to install nuclear cruise missiles, exactly as at Greenham. The seeds of the beginnings of a women's peace camp were being sown and a major international protest was being planned in Sicily to coincide with March 8th, which was International Women's Day. I quickly asked if I could come to Sicily too. I wanted to escape Brenda and I wanted a completely new environment.

I came out of prison on Tuesday and yet on the Saturday, having rushed back to the camp and collected a sleeping bag and some clothes that I left there before going inside, I was on a plane with three other Greenham women flying to Palermo in Sicily. Bizarrely, the flight was with Air India, and we flew over in a gigantic jumbo jet. This was now my second flight in less than four months. Prior to becoming involved in Greenham Common, I had only been on a plane once, when I was seven and had gone to Paris.

When we arrived, the warm air hit us and I felt I was far away from England, it was so hot, I removed my jacket. In Palermo, there were palm trees and beautiful old castle-like buildings all around.

We looked for somewhere to eat and came across a restaurant. We were unprepared for the reaction we got. When we opened the door, and walked in, everyone stopped talking and stared. The restaurant was for men only, or so it seemed. Only waiters no waitresses, we stood our ground though and then sat at a table and we were served though we were stared at continuously which made us uncomfortable. The men in the restaurant were clearly not used to women eating out alone, or eating out at all perhaps.

Later we travelled by train to the south of Sicily to Comiso, which was a small town close to an American air base. The train rattled along in the sunshine extremely slowly. We passed orange trees, which I'd never seen before. I felt the urge to stick my arm out and try and grab an orange. I felt a million miles away from Holloway.

After disembarking at Comiso, we started to walk up the road in the sweltering heat to look for the restaurant where we had been told other peace activist women would be. Trouble was that a group of

A New Man

about fifteen boys also got off the train at the same time. Clearly, they were unused to seeing women on their own on the streets, or maybe they could tell we were vulnerable foreigners, as they began to harass us...physically. They were like a swarm attacking the four of us. They touched us all over and grabbed us in-between our legs. It was hopeless trying to fend them off. I felt disgusted and violated.

We persevered up the hill, trying to bat them away. Then we saw a bar and dived into it presuming the boys wouldn't follow. They didn't. In the bar that we tried to obtain refuge in, all the staff were male. They weren't particularly bothered when we tried to ask for assistance. Then we saw a woman on the street and we rushed to her asking where the restaurant was, Fortunately, she was also going to the restaurant where all the peace women were and so she took us there.

We entered the room at the back of the restaurant and our arrival from Greenham Common was announced. This was the cue for all the women there to start singing the well-known Greenham Song 'You can't kill the sprit, she is like a mountain, she goes on and on'. Most of us had by now got sick to the teeth with this song but it was different to hear it here in Sicily in this situation and be welcomed by all these women. In the room, we met women from Holland, Denmark, Switzerland as well as from Italy and Sicily.

It was decided that a blockade of the base would take place. Sicily was very different to England. The Carabinieri, the military police, fired over the heads of a group of women who were only walking around the planned nuclear base. This didn't inspire confidence; nevertheless, the next day the planned blockade of the base started quite well. There were a group of us who sat in the road thereby preventing all traffic entering the base.

The police were called to assist and they were very rough. They pulled us away, some women were pulled away by their hair and then the police held us down until all the traffic which had queued up was able to pass by. Then they would let us go. We immediately returned to the road again to blockade. This happened a few times, but each time the police got more violent.

Escaping to Holloway Prison

The blockade wasn't managing to stop the traffic and the violence was escalating so I left the blockage of my own accord. I didn't want to get injured. I sat in the nearby caravan with others who had come to the same conclusion. A Swiss woman, Sarina, joined me soon after. Her arm had been hurt from the rough treatment. We encouraged others to end the blockade but many were determined to keep trying. Then, without warning, the remaining women on the blockade were arrested and driven off in vans.

They were taken to a medieval-looking prison twelve miles away in Ragusa. Sarina and a British woman both had their arms broken by the police. Sarina could speak English and Italian as well as her own Swiss German language which was obviously very handy. She was tall, thin, wore glasses and had a serious but compassionate and friendly demeanour.

She was also a good writer. She was writing a piece for the swiss peace movement from Comiso and detailing the action but now with her right arm damaged and in plaster she couldn't write at all, but she looked on the funny side of things. 'Can you believe it? The bank won't accept my signature because I can't write as I normally do,' she told me in her endearing Swiss accent. I agreed it was pretty ridiculous.

The camp hadn't been properly set up yet so we stayed in empty houses in Comiso. These were empty houses with nothing in them except for bed frames and mattresses. I'm guessing that they were squats or simply empty properties that no one wanted. One night, when we were in one of these rooms, after spending time with Sarina over a bottle of wine, I kissed her and she kissed back. There were others in the room and one woman told us to be quiet, so that's all that happened but we developed an attachment.

Days went by, we desperately tried to extract information from the Sicilian authorities as to what was going to happen with the women who were still detained. I didn't know if they would be released in time to catch the plane back to England or not. I wanted to fly back with everyone after they had been released. It didn't feel right leaving them behind in Sicily. But the day of our return flight came and went and

A New Man

then later we heard that they had all been deported.

There were two Greenham women who had not been involved in the action and they were staying in another Sicilian city, Catania. I went to see them to request some Greenham money so that I could get back to England but my return journey had now changed though, because Sarina, had invited me back to Switzerland to visit.

Being a woman alone in Sicily did not appeal in the slightest and I was glad to be leaving. Only that afternoon, we had gone out walking in Catania and the traffic had come to a standstill when four of us were just walking on the pavement minding our own business. Car drivers screed to a halt. It was alarming. Men started shouting at us from the car windows and tooting their horns.

Sarina suggested running down a side street. So, we ran as fast as we could. One car started following us and we only managed to give him the slip by darting into a square. We got back indoors as soon as we could. It was too distressing.

I found spending time with Sarina reassuring and a comfort. She appeared caring, gentle and an intelligent woman, very much an intellectual. She was ten years older than me, 27, tall with brown hair and wore glasses, an academic. She seemed to have sufficient money at her disposal through her sporadic work. Of course, her language abilities were invaluable. She seemed remarkably unbothered about her broken arm but she was keen to get back home. I was delighted she had offered me the opportunity to go back with her to Switzerland and to have a break from peace activism.

10

The Swiss Dream

I'll never forget the journey by train from Sicily to Switzerland. It was deeply romantic and the scenery was stunning. I was weary and recovering from the ordeal of Holloway prison and the unhappy relationship with Brenda but then I was transported to another world, a much more secure and beautiful world.

Sarina and I were going to catch the train all the way up through Italy to the very north of Switzerland. First, we went to a grocery shop in Catania and bought some bread and cheese for the journey. In the train carriage, we sat opposite each other and looked intently into each other's eyes. I felt secure and calm.

We had to spend a night in the station waiting room in Milan for a connection in the morning which wasn't very comfortable but was bearable. It was cold and there was a lot of snoring from the other waiting room residents. But then the next day made up for it as the scenery got more and more beautiful as we came up to the Alps.

It was mid-March so there was a still lot of snow on the mountains. Sarina explained to me how we would go round and round the lake to get higher and higher through the Alps and through the tunnel through to Switzerland. Having not travelled at all, I was in complete awe of the beauty of the snow and the mountains. Finally, late in the evening, we arrived in Schaffhausen in the very north of Switzerland. Schaffhausen was pronounced by the locals in their swiss dialect as 'shaffooza' rather than in standard German, 'shaffhowzen'.

We stopped for a snack and a drink in the railway cafeteria. This was more like a posh restaurant than the railways cafes I was used to in England; it was immaculately clean and quiet with low warm soothing lighting. We then had to catch a smaller commuter train to a tiny village called Beringen, which is where Sarina lived.

A New Man

We entered her little cottage and I sat down in her little front room by a small round table with a white lace tablecloth. Sarina poured out two glasses of red wine and then we kissed lightly and gently. We had arrived. I overflowed with relief. Here there were no soldiers or police to worry about, no shouting, no aggression and no insecurities. There was only peace and silence. I was safe. The cottage could have come out of a fairy tale. I felt emotional, and tears fell onto the white lace table cloth.

The next few days were luxurious. I felt like I'd landed in a bed of feathers and I revelled in the comfort. The local people were very friendly; everyone would greet everyone else saying 'Grüezi mitenand' which translated to 'Greetings one and all'. I could understand a bit of Swiss German from my school lessons and I liked the Swiss German dialect. It reminded me slightly of Welsh or Dutch in that it was much more melodic. I started to learn some Swiss words and quickly felt a connection to Switzerland.

I felt at peace and I finally started to properly relax, something I hadn't done in a very long time. I was away from the missiles, the soldiers, the ever-present threat of evictions, the difficulties in keeping dry and warm, away from other women's problems and heavy conversations.

Sarina was heterosexual until she met me. She said she'd started looking at women differently since meeting me. The advantage of this for me was that she had no experience of lesbian sex. But my behaviour did not match her expectations and she spent a lot of time comparing me with men. She said that I behaved like a man sexually. Perhaps this was because I preferred tribadism, which for want of a better term is effectively lesbian dry humping, and I wouldn't let her touch my breasts. I also didn't like her touching me between my legs, especially because being inexperienced she curled her finger and her nail hurt me. I should've said, of course, but I didn't want to upset her.

We visited some of the sights such as the waterfall of the Rhine nearby and Zurich. The air was fresh and clear and there was very little noise. I loved how clean, tidy and efficient everything was. As soon as

I put some ash in an ash tray in a restaurant it was whisked away by a waiter. The trams were incredibly frequent too, arriving every six minutes. Life was measured and unhurried. I felt I could get used to this way of life. After about two weeks, I had to go back to England as Sarina was due to go to Vienna. We didn't make any plans for the future.

I didn't feel like returning to Greenham Common particularly but I didn't have anywhere else to go. As it was cheaper, I planned to go back to England by train and coach and to stop off in Amsterdam to see Justina on the way back.

I said goodbye to Sarina at Zurich railway station and it was exceptionally emotional. Railway station partings brought back sad memories at the best of times but this was particularly hard. I didn't want to leave her.

Just as I was about to climb up the stairs to board the train she handed me a chocolate Easter bunny which brought tears to my eyes. The train left the station and I felt I'd lost someone who properly cared. My guts hurt from the emotional pain, I felt like I'd been punched in the stomach. The other people in the carriage stared at me because I could not stop sobbing.

The journey took all night. It was very crowded on the train and I didn't get much sleep. The next morning, just after ten I walked out of central station in Amsterdam into the bright piercing sunshine.

I looked up my sister's address in my address book. Then to my shock, I realised that I didn't have her actual door number, only the street name. There was nothing for it, but just to walk to her street and then knock on every single door and ask if anyone knew a 'Justina Kiss' I did this about fifteen times, when amazingly a man replied that he did know her and he pointed out to me where she lived just a few doors along.

I rang the bell and her head poked out of the window.

'Hello, what are you doing here?' She said. She seemed delighted and came downstairs to let me in. Over a cup of tea, I carefully explained all what happened with the deportations. 'And now I'm on my way back to England.' I said.

A New Man

It was good to see her. I felt welcomed and secure in her company.

'How did you afford all the travelling costs?' she asked

'Oh, it came out of Greenham funds.'

'Well, they certainly look after you, don't they!'

This was true, I had my travelling costs covered but I didn't feel especially looked after. Although the intentions were there, Greenham was far too anarchistic and busy to be able to look after people properly, especially a young person. There was no membership scheme, no structure, there didn't even exist a clear definition of a Greenham Woman. At Greenham, if you didn't ask, you didn't get.

Justina was very generous to me for the few days I was in Amsterdam. I felt comforted having a sister. She took me to bars and cafes and introduced me to her friends. We talked a bit about our respective different experiences growing up. Justina was still vegetarian and I wasn't, that division remained. I enjoyed the stay in Amsterdam and then it was time to leave. I caught the cheap coach back to England.

Back in England, I returned to Greenham. I walked into the local pub, 'The Rokeby Arms' and met some other Greenham women playing pool. I was told that the very next day there was another mass action planned. A mass blockade of the base was planned with CND.

I didn't take any part of this myself though as I was still trying to re-orientate myself. It felt uncomfortable being back at the camp. I felt a lot tension since I had ended the unpleasant relationship with Brenda. Other women still didn't understand how much the experience had affected me but then of course they all had their own lives and worries as well as maintaining the camp and the campaign.

There had been discussion about plans for a book to be published about the camp. To contribute to this, I decided to go away for a while to write about my experiences. I travelled to Marta's new place. She had moved to Weston Super Mare and I started to write for the book there. Some of my writing was eventually published in a book on Greenham Common entitled 'Women at the Wire'

It probably would have been better if Sarina and I hadn't kept on writing to each other but we did. She wrote that I could have gone with her to Vienna. She hadn't suggested it at the time though and I didn't have the money to go in any case. I sent Sarina the best book on Britain I could find. I chose a large colour book on British countryside partly out of pride as she said she had no interest in coming to Britain.

I started receiving letters back, very romantic letters explaining to me that she missed me. She then wrote to me and told me she was in love with me. Then when I told her I was writing for a book about Greenham Common, she suggested that I go to Switzerland to write.

I wasn't sure what was for the best but I decided to follow my heart and return to Switzerland. I caught the train and arrived in Beringen in late April. Sarina had told me before I left England that she would be staying for the summer up an alp which I was keen to do.

We were in her living room in Beringen when she told me the bloke who would be going up the alp was also an ex-boyfriend of hers and he might not be keen on me accompanying them. I was shocked. Why the hell didn't she explain this before? This was going to be disastrous and I was beginning to think this has been a wasted journey. She said it might be okay though. I was doubtful.

I was right. Billy, the ex-boyfriend, said at a meal right in front of us, that he didn't like English people and that he didn't want me to come with them. So, that was that. This time I was really fed up having to go back to England.

That night Sarina laid on top of me and held me close all night while I sobbed. I was so distraught at the mess of it and angry at Billy. How stupid and ignorant I thought, of him to announce, 'I don't like English people.'

What had Sarina ever seen in the obnoxious man? Sarina tried to reassure me, 'I'll only be up the alp for six months,' she protested.

'Six months!' I gasped, 'That's ages away. There's no way I can't wait for you that long.'

So much for organising an anti-nuclear action in Switzerland, which had been another plan. I couldn't wait another six months for her. I returned to England by coach again, dejected, and back yet again, to Greenham Common.

A New Man

I didn't know what to do next. I thought of going to Berlin with Sally, a woman from the camp, as it was an exciting city I was keen to visit but we established quickly that we were not going to get on. She was a serious vegan, I was a meat eater and she refused to spend any time with someone who ate burgers, so that was a non-starter.

Surprisingly, though the letters from Sarina continued. Sarina was not, it turned out, enjoying her time with Billy up in the alp. She wrote she was thinking of leaving but I felt like she was teasing me. I should have cut contact there and then.

Meanwhile there were further actions taking place at other military bases throughout England. On one of these actions at a four-day blockade of the Upper Heyford air force base, near Oxford, I met a lovely woman called Rebekah. She was shorter than me, had shoulder-length blond hair and twinkling blue eyes. She was very friendly and warm. We hit it off immediately and had a mutual instant attraction. So much so, that we spontaneously held hands and touched each other without any awkwardness, and then later I gave her a piggy back along the fence. When the blockade had finished, I just couldn't bring myself to say goodbye to her and return to Greenham. So, I just stayed with her and went back to London with the whole group she'd some with in an old ambulance. I wasn't so bold as to ask if I could stay over with her so I stayed over in a spare room of another woman's in Islington. When I woke up, I went downstairs and I saw two notes saying that Rebekah had rang for me and to contact her. Excited, I called her up and we arranged to meet up near the Angel.

By coincidence, the doors of the ambulance had jammed and no one could open them so I was unable to retrieve my rucksack that I carried everywhere I went. This was the perfect excuse to stay longer in London with Rebekah and consequently we had a great few days together. We went out to a large new lesbian club called 'The Bell' in King's Cross. We got close, danced and kissed passionately up against the juke box.

That week, Thursday 9th June 1983, was the General Election. I wasn't registered anywhere to vote unfortunately in the aftermath of the Falklands War, the Conservatives won the election. Things seemed desperate. At this point, Labour had a manifesto to do the right thing, to remove nuclear weapons from our land, so there was great dismay amongst us that the Conservatives had won again.

A few days later, I was at Rebekah's when I got a phone call from Corrie at the camp at Greenham.

'There's a telegram for you,' Corrie said.

'Really! my god, I'd never had a telegram before, can you open it for me please and read it out?' I asked.

'Sure,.....,it says, "Left the alp. Arrive in Britain around June 17 Love Sarina." Do you want me to post it to you?'

'No, don't bother, thanks' I replied, 'I'll be down at Greenham by the time it would get here.'

I could not believe it. I was stunned and disorientated. It was Tuesday and June 17th was the Friday. I had started coming to terms with the idea that I would never see Sarina again and I had pushed all thoughts about her to the back of my mind and now I had met Rebekah too. I knew things weren't going so well for Sarina but I didn't for one moment think she'd leave the alp and come to England.

I felt obligated to drop everything and go and spend time with Sarina. I thought I had no choice but to end things with Rebekah too and to go back to Greenham immediately and await Sarina's arrival, though I had completely mixed feelings about seeing her again. I was also anxious that Sarina should get a good impression of Britain. It was now my turn to show her my country.

Sarina arrived at the camp on the Saturday. I had been getting tense waiting for her. Her arrival was just before the 'Dragon Festival' was due to take place. The 'Dragon' was a long patchwork of different women's tapestry/banner work to be joined together. This was planned to be a mythological symbolic demonstration and one I didn't feel inspired by in the slightest.

Nevertheless, because it was a major event, visitors from London came down and I was very pleased to discover that Rebekah had also come down again in the ambulance vehicle. I got in it, at the main

A New Man

gate camp and ended up staying in it with Rebekah while it was driven around the camp. I felt such a strong magnetic attraction to Rebekah, it was uncanny.

Sarina quite liked the camp but I don't think it was organised enough for her and she had many questions. A woman then arrived at the camp who was quite aggressive, picking arguments with people and kicking things. Unfortunately, this woman used similar phrases to me, like 'You know what I mean' and we wore similar clothes, which Sarina picked up on. I wore a black motorcycle jacket and motorcycle boots and this woman dressed similarly.

Sarina started comparing me with this woman and I was offended by her sudden criticism of me. She said I was lazy, not self-critical enough, that I didn't know what I wanted to do in life, and that I was self-destructive, masculine and aggressive.

From telling me she loved me very much and how wonderful I was, she had changed her opinion of me quite dramatically. I didn't reel out a list of Sarina's imperfections. I knew I had faults and some of what she said was true but I protested that no way was I as aggressive as this woman and I was right. Later she held a knife to a woman and threatened sexual assault. Having no doors to shut, no boundary, meant that there were often visitors who came to Greenham with their own problems.

I suggested to Sarina that we leave right away and explore Britain as that had been the plan anyway. We went first to stay at my mum's, then we had a full weekend in London. Rebecca, who I had gone to Norway with, kindly allowed us to stay in her flat in Old Street and this enabled me to show Sarina the lesbian clubs in London, The Carved Red Lion and The Bell. We also visited the feminist bookshop in Islington, 'Sisterwrite.' I showed her Hampstead Heath and we went to the cinema. I was determined to give her a good time in London and show her that Britain wasn't this terrible place she had thought it was.

After London, we hitchhiked to The Gower area in Wales. We visited castles, beaches and mountains going right up to the north of Wales. Because we depended on men giving us lifts, I felt painfully inadequate and I wished that I had enough money to learn to drive and have a car and be able to drive Sarina around. At least the change of scenery was welcome, however, and the relationship between us seemed to recover a bit.

Sarina was surprised that in Britain there were parts that spoke a different language and was frustrated with me that I couldn't fully explain the constitutional arrangement England had with Wales. I felt useless as Sarina's intellectualism dwarfed mine. She said I should be embarrassed that she knew English words that I didn't. My education just hadn't been as good as hers.

After Wales, we hitch hiked through England to York, where I intended to show Sarina where I'd spent time growing up. We arrived very late at night and definitely too late at four in the morning to ask a friend to put us up for the night. It started raining heavily and we attempted to shelter under some big old trees near the racecourse. Sarina was shivering badly from the cold. I felt terrible at not being able to provide better shelter and couldn't wait so at 6.30am I woke up a friend who was not pleased at all.

During the last few days of the tour of Britain, it was obvious that the relationship was not working. We were arguing too much and her opinion of me also nose-dived. We said goodbye at Victoria Coach Station a month after her first arriving at Greenham. As soon as we said goodbye I felt an immense sense of relief. This was now finally over and I had tried my best. Sooner than it was decent, I phoned Rebekah to see if she was around as I was back in London.

11

Leaving Greenham

I had lost much motivation for Greenham and the continuing actions. Campaigning and the basic living at the camp was exhausting. I needed some time away or to leave the camp. Time away in Switzerland had been a break but it had not been enough. I was burnt out, and needed to recharge myself but I wasn't sure of what I should do.

I felt drawn to London as that's where I started out in life and it was a city of possibilities, especially for lesbians. I stayed with Rebekah and we went out a lot and had fun. We went to see the band 'The Poison Girls', a band that had supported CRASS and a feminist punk duo called 'Toxic Shock' in Hackney.

Things moved fast with Rebekah and we fell in love. There was one very big problem though and that was that Rebekah was just starting to get much more involved in the campaign at Greenham Common at precisely the time I wanted to have less to do with it. I wanted to move to London, so she agreed that I would stay with her temporarily until I found somewhere to live.

Rebekah worked as a volunteer at the London Greenham Office in Old Street, promoting and advertising actions at the camp and in London. She had also been arrested at the first major blockade when work first started to build the cruise missile silos in Easter 1982. However, she now wanted to spend practically all her time living at the camp itself.

At least now the camps had multiplied. Right at the beginning of the year there was an idea to spread camps out from the only two permanent camps, the main one and the camp close to the silos. There were predictably some conflicts in such close living arrangements and on a practical level more space was needed due to the increase in numbers of women staying there. So, other camps were created. They were named after the colours of the rainbow initially and then after these were used other colours were used such as turquoise. These different camps developed their own identities. For example, the Blue Gate Camp was known as strictly vegan. The Green Gate Camp, which was very close to the cruise missile silos was more spiritual and strongly separatist. It was hidden from view in the trees. This was where Brenda mostly stayed and I steered well clear.

The Orange Gate Camp was close to the start of the runway on the east side and Rebekah moved there. I inevitably ended up spending time at the camp to be with Rebekah but I found myself getting depressed. I was bored with the discussions, tired of the discomfort and I loathed the camp fire and its continual smoke. I was only there for Rebekah and much preferred being in London.

To celebrate my 18th birthday, as we didn't have much money we went to our favourite café in Kentish Town. Rebekah bought me a trifle which was my favourite desert. Even though it wasn't much, it was special.

Now that I was 18, Dad wrote to let me know that he was stopping the monthly payments of £50 into my bank account which had been a huge help for the two years since leaving home.

I attempted to sign on the following week to obtain unemployment benefit in London with Rebekah's encouragement as my income was now precisely zero. The man behind the counter asked me what work I could do and I didn't know what to say. After a few moments, I said that I could do painting and decorating. He wasn't impressed but duly filled out the forms. I didn't have a clue of what work I wanted to do, what was available nor what I was capable of. There was no guidance or help offered to me.

I received a letter telling me I wasn't entitled to unemployment benefit a few days later which worried me sick. I bumped into Toni, outside the Sisterwrite bookshop shortly afterwards though and she told me that this letter was automatic and that I should still get some money in the form of 'supplementary benefit' which was confusing but somewhat reassuring. Sure enough, a few days later I received confirma-

A New Man

tion that I would be getting some money to live on-the supplementary benefit.

I visited Rebekah's family. Coincidentally, it transpired that Rebekah's dad was an artist as well and he had taught my dad at the Central School of Art. Rebekah's sister was getting married so there was a lot of activity in all the preparations when I visited. They were very welcoming to me and it was lovely to feel almost part of their family. I was in love with Rebekah and I wanted us to marry and have children. If only it had been possible then.

In August I got my first ever dole cheque. I spent it all on a bike. Rebekah wasn't impressed with this as I'd been staying with her and owed her money for food etc. But I was sure it would be worth it in the long run, having a bike and saving on public transport costs.

We planned to go to Amsterdam in late August to spend some time with Justina to have a bit of a holiday before going on to Geneva in Switzerland. In Geneva, high-level disarmament talks between the US and Russia were taking place to try and reach agreement on the Strategic Arms Limitation Treaty and actions were planned there. In Amsterdam, we stayed with Justina for a few days and visited the famous old Amsterdam sytle Lesbian bar there, 'Cafe Saarein' with Justina.

In order to get to Switzerland, the plan was to hitch through Germany but when we were hitchhiking we had a nasty experience. A man had stopped to pick up a lone woman hitchhiker but he wasn't going her way so we got in instead. He drove fast and I studied the map, charting our progress and was thrilled that we would get there in no time. I was in the front as I could speak a bit of German, Rebekah was in the back seat. To my horror, I saw that the driver was moving his hand up and down fast. I had been so absorbed in the map, I didn't notice for ages that he was masturbating.

I turned to Rebekah and said, 'He's wanking!'

'Tell him to stop the car and let us out right now,' Rebekah replied.

I couldn't remember the words in German then suddenly they came to me, and I spoke as calmly and assertively as I could. He complied and drove us into a service station. Rebekah warned me to get out at the same time as her, in case of child locks. Once we were out and he had driven off, we were grateful nothing worse had happened but we were both felt awful.

But now we were stuck in the middle of Germany with very little money so we had no option but to continue hitching. Next to come along was a mini bus. A young man let us on board and he took us to his parents'; there, we were fed and even given a bed for the night. We were now very close to Geneva and only needed one more lift in the morning, which passed without incident. We made a decision that we would never hitch again, even if it meant not travelling anywhere due to lack of money as the risks were just too great.

When we arrived in Geneva, we met up with other Greenham women and women from the camp in Sicily and Sarina was there too. It was strange seeing Sarina there but things weren't unpleasant. There was a blockading action of the UN building but we didn't feel like joining in. Afterwards, we had a lift through the night all the way back and we were both pleased to be returning to London, it had not been much of a holiday.

Rebekah started spending a lot more time at Greenham and was forging strong friendships. Another action then took place and I Joined in. This action was a momentous one. It was agreed and passed on by word of mouth only that on 29th October at 4pm exactly we would start cutting down the 9-mile perimeter fence of the base with bolt cutters. The action took the police by complete surprise and they were unprepared. In less than five minutes four miles of the nine-mile fence came down.

Whilst I was cutting the ties of the fence to the concrete post, I was pulled away roughly from the fence by a policeman. A policewoman on my other side held my other arm and asked the policeman to be careful with me. He then told her, extremely irritated, that she was as bad as us. You could see that sometimes our approach aggravated gender divisions.

I was arrested but released without charge, as was Rebekah and many others. Either they couldn't cope with the numbers or they had

A New Man

changed tactic to minimise media coverage because being arrested to stop activities and then released without being charged started to happen more often.

A big CND demonstration at the camp followed two days later, on 31st October. Things were getting very tense as the nuclear missiles were due to arrive any day. Sarah Tisdall, a civil servant had only a week earlier leaked the arrival date of the missiles to the Guardian newspaper as being 1st November 1983. The leak resulted in her going to Holloway prison for four months as the Guardian was forced to reveal their source.

At Greenham, we waited and waited. But because of the leak, the arrival of the cruise missiles was delayed and they eventually arrived on Monday 14th November 1983. There wasn't any notification, we just saw them the exact moment the colossal planes with the nuclear missiles on board were flown in.

It was incredibly upsetting. I was distraught that after everything we had done, after everything we had been through that we had failed to stop the missiles coming to the country. A red lumpy rash appeared all over my body the day the same day, clearly a strong psychosomatic response to the missiles arriving as the rash disappeared after a day. I was thoroughly deflated. I wanted to leave the camp, and to try and forget everything. I wanted to live in a house again, stop stinking of camp smoke and to stop being recognised everywhere I went as a 'Greenham Woman'. I wanted to live a normal life.

To my mind the fight was lost. But others felt very differently. Many Greenham Women stayed and they fought in the courts and they continued with actions. Their aim, which I thought was ridiculously far-fetched, was not only to remove nuclear missiles but also to return the military base back to common land usage, which is what it had been before the British military requisitioned the land.

"Cruise Watch" started and this was a network of people that tracked the missiles when they left the base and this was successful in bringing to people's attention that nuclear missiles were bring driven around their streets and sometimes they'd manage to disrupt the movement of the missiles.

A case was brought where two Greenham women asserted that the byelaws created by the MOD were in fact contrary to the more ancient common land law and this took over two years, going all the way to the House of Lords before reaching its conclusion in their favour. In 1997, six years after the last missiles had gone, Newbury council bought back its common land from the Ministry of Defence for the sum of £7 Million. Greenham Common women, to my amazement and respect, achieved their stated aim of returning the military land back to the common people.

The protest invigorated and empowered women to protest. Greenham women were involved in countless actions thereafter including the action when lesbians abseiled in the House of Lords and disrupted BBC news to protest the homophobic Clause 28 proposed law at the time (which was passed) designed to prevent teachers from speaking or teaching about lesbianism and homosexuality.

For me though, it was time to establish myself away from Greenham, to be someone other than a Greenham woman. This was much easier said than done. I tried to stay in London most of the time, which was the obvious first step to leaving Greenham, psychologically as well as socially but I struggled about where I fitted in the world and my identity.

My inner conflict around masculinity and femininity now had space to reassert itself as I was alone in the flat in London and no longer affected by other women's issues, actions, police, etc. I had trouble sleeping. I thought about why it was that warmongers were usually men. Was it 'natural' for men to be the aggressors? Or was it just that they were in the powerful positions. Would women really be better than men if they were country rulers? and why were men the enemy exactly? Why did so many women go out with men, if they were so awful?

I wanted to stay in the flat, as a cocoon from the outside world. I was so tired, I often woke up at midday despite going to sleep at midnight. I didn't like having to go out, instead I took to worshipping Rebekah's

A New Man

flat and I cleaned and hoovered. It was like a palace to me. Rebekah, however, had only been offered the flat to me as a temporary place to stay. I needed to find somewhere else to live. I called up, answering adverts for lodgers I'd seen in various feminist newsletters.

The trouble was that practically the first question they asked of me was, 'What do you do?' I had no answer to this as I hadn't settled or worked out yet what I was going to do. I just answered honestly that I had left Greenham and was now looking for somewhere to live. This didn't go down well at all. Despite lesbians and feminists advertising rooms, I wasn't suitable because I didn't have a job or a place at college.

My priority was to leave Greenham, find somewhere to live and then get myself sorted. But all these women who rented out rooms wanted me sorted first with a job or a college place. I wasn't getting anywhere.

12

Breakdown

I had been looking for somewhere to live for weeks unsuccessfully when I had a panic attack. It was a Friday in early January. I was standing on the platform at Kentish Town tube with Rebekah. I suddenly had rushing feelings go up and down my spine. I was confused and frightened. I felt like I quickly had to do something, anything. I had the urge to jump onto the tracks.

Rebekah didn't know what was going on, as I was behaving strangely and walking back and forth, 'What's the matter?' she asked.

'I don't know, I don't know,' was all I could muster.

'Let's get outside,' she said.

We got out of the tube station. Rebekah was very worried about me. The intense physical feelings of acute alarm subsided but I was freaked out by what had happened. It made me unsure of myself.

It was now a new year: 1984. I felt under more pressure to find somewhere to live but after this panic attack my confidence suffered. I wasn't in a fit state to organise anything. When I got on a bus I fumbled for money to give the driver and I realised with horror that I'd forgotten how to count out change. I felt pathetic as there were some school children in front of me who worked it out effortlessly but my brain had slowed to a stop.

After the panic attack, Rebekah decided to allow me to have my own room in her flat a bit longer, until I'd got myself together. I was pleased. I was also able to sign up to subscriptions to all the newsletters that I wanted such as the weekly 'London Women's Liberation Newsletter' and the internationalist feminist publication 'Outwrite'.

I rang Marta. We hadn't really talked since a miserable Christmas when we didn't even get it together to cook a Christmas meal.

'I've got somewhere to stay, at least temporarily. I can stay here at

A New Man

Rebekah's'.

Marta replied, 'That is really good news. Now you can get on with things and do something.'

'What do you mean, do something?' I felt pressurised. Even though I wasn't doing much on the face of things, I didn't feel well enough to do anything.

'Just do something, like a class, driving lessons, even a job, just as long as you DO something.' Marta said, emphatically.

I signed up for a course of driving lessons, not in the right frame of mind at all to embark on this. I went along to a women-only carpentry lesson too but I found it too hard so I didn't return. Rebekah meanwhile reported that the activities had become much more serious at Greenham. In this latest determined attempt to remove the women permanently from outside the base, evictions were carried out daily, sometimes three times a day, seven days a week, and these were horrendous. Bailiffs would arrive at about six in the morning and they collected everything they could including tents, food, clothes and all manner of personal possessions and chucked everything seized into the awaiting 'munchers', the rubbish vans.

The bailiffs would then put out the camp fire with a fire extinguisher. The camp was then cleared and the bailiffs moved on to the next camp. The trick to circumvent this was to get everything in cars before they arrived, drive off nearby and then return after the bailiffs had gone and set up camp again. The blue camp would get the bailiffs first, being the nearest camp to the town Newbury, so someone from the blue camp would have to try and quickly alert the others to get prepared. As this was long before the days of mobile phones this meant driving round (or cycling sometimes if no car was available) as quickly as possible to all the other camps alerting everyone that they were on their way. Sometimes it worked well but inevitably many personal possessions were taken and the atmosphere was frantic and it was exhausting.

Soldiers, it seemed, were given free rein to cause havoc from within the base too. The 'paras' were reportedly particularly violent. They threw bricks and metal stakes at the benders. With this going on and

Greenham becoming so unpleasant. I became very worried about Rebekah and desperately wanted her to give up the fight and return to London, where she would be safe. I wanted to dissociate myself from Greenham completely and I yearned to live a more normal life with some security with Rebekah, the woman I loved. Rebekah, on the other hand, was totally committed to Greenham and felt totally unsupported by me amid this severe harassment from the bailiffs. Our worlds were becoming more separate.

My personal identity crisis then came to a head when I discovered some Penthouse magazines left by a previous lodger in the flat. Looking at them, I became incredibly turned on. I'd never seen such exciting sexual images of women. I had a powerful orgasm, better than I'd ever experienced but afterwards I didn't feel good at all. Instead I felt ridden with guilt.

I had fantasised I was a man with the women in the pictures. My enjoyment of these images conflicted with the feminist beliefs I had subscribed to. In my diary, I had written on the inside cover:

'Pornography = Death, Racism, Sexism, Murder and Hatred'

I believed that images of naked women were presented for men's benefit and that pornography was oppressive, violent and exploitative. How could anyone possibly enjoy it? And yet I had just done precisely that. I was just like a man. I had a penis, at least in my head, and nuclear missiles were phallic symbols. Penises were therefore equated with the most awful thing imaginable. Categorically, then, I was also evil.

Disgusted and horrified with myself I proceeded to destroy every single magazine, cutting each page into quarters. I was seriously faulty:

I was very male and everything I shouldn't be.

I should think like a woman but I didn't. I started to think about all the things I didn't like about Greenham Common. I didn't like the habitual hugging of everyone whether you knew them or not. I disliked the euphemistically called 'non-hierarchical' set up (because hierarchies still existed) and I preferred structures and order. The so called 'non-hierarchical' set-up simply made it easier for the more confident women to do what they wanted to and the lack of structure meant decision making was exhausting. I knew I was much more comfortable in an organised methodical setting; the lack of structure and endless emotional meetings didn't suit me. I yearned for structure and security.

I also knew that I quite liked uniforms, which was unthinkable. If you think what masculinity often stereotypically conveys, I concluded that I fitted neatly into the stereotypical masculine box and I suddenly saw that I was on the wrong side of the fence at Greenham.

There is now in most feminist circles a more nuanced appraisal of what masculine means and there is an idea of female masculinity of course but in the early 1980s within women only groups and Greenham Common circles everything was very black and white and it was a destabilising shock realising I was on the dark side. Masculinity was regularly put down by practically everyone around me so I could hardly talk to anyone about it. No wonder I supressed the feelings. I was at a loss as to how I should continue.

I couldn't do sex anymore. There were too many decisions complicated by associations of maleness and femaleness in my head. I lost any natural instinctive sensual and sexual desires and instead was rigid with fear and indecision about what was acceptable and the symbolism of body parts and positions. I couldn't relax and I certainly couldn't reveal to anyone my dark shameful secret: that I felt male.

It seemed the only option would be first to find and then assert my womanhood, my femininity. Facing this awareness of my masculinity, my only conclusion was that it was time I learnt how to behave as a woman. I also thought it would help to distance myself from the butch lesbian image. My first step was to wear eyeliner for the first time in my life and I bought a handbag. This didn't make me feel more confident though, it had the opposite effect. I didn't really know who I was and what kind of image fitted me best. Everything was being re-evaluated from scratch and it was difficult to know where to start.

One evening I went to Rebekah's regular pub in Islington, the Island Queen, in my 'new woman' role. It didn't go well. I was thinking too much and I could barely utter a sentence and felt useless. I disintegrated there on the bar stool holding my new handbag, wearing eyeliner. I was nervous and I stuttered when Rebekah's friends tried to talk to me. I returned dejected to the flat and wished I hadn't ventured out.

The more insecure I became, the needier I was but I was also very reluctant to appear needy so I did my best to hide this but then this gave the impression of me being aloof and uncaring. Rebekah began to get the impression that I was using her, just so that I could stay in London and she concluded she didn't want me at the flat anymore. With Rebekah at Greenham and me in London, we weren't spending much time together so she couldn't see how I was deteriorating. It was always a temporary arrangement in any case. So, she asked me to leave.

This was an absolute disaster for me as I wasn't in a fit state to leave.

'I can't leave, I have nowhere to go.' I said.

'You can always stay at the Greenham house.' Rebekah said.

'I can't go there, it's awful, messy and chaotic with different women staying over all the time and full of Greenham women.' I replied.

It was the very last place I wanted to go. I wanted to avoid Greenham women in my quest for a new identity. I walked out of the flat to get some air and to think but when I returned there was a note on the sideboard from Rebekah saying I had to leave.

I turned up at Marta's place without warning and could barely explain myself. I just showed her Rebekah's note. Marta had moved from Weston-Super-Mare to a tiny one-room bedsit in Bristol. All this time wherever Marta had moved, she had always had tried to keep a room for me, just in case. Now I needed one, there wasn't one available. I agonised over what was acceptable for a human being to have. What was it reasonable for me to have? I had lost sight of what I needed and what I wanted.

Having lived at Greenham, I knew that you didn't need four walls, a carpet, furniture, a TV, electricity, even. I couldn't fathom a way to be. I just saw a fragile structure to justify our consumerist lives. I knew I needed stability but I didn't know how to get it. Where should I go and what on earth was I entitled to have and what was reasonable and fair to expect?

Marta was quite low at this point as she had very little money and

A New Man

was now signing on having given up her job in Weston-Super-Mare due to a teacher sexually harassing her. That evening we went for a walk and walked past the famous Bristol Suspension Bridge. We half joked about throwing ourselves over the edge together. Not unusual as they have Samaritans telephone numbers on signs of either side of the bridge but we hadn't quite reached that point yet.

When I returned to London four days later, I discovered a squat just a ten-minute bike ride away from Rebekah's had been opened by a mutual friend of ours so finally I moved out of Rebekah's flat. I didn't even ask them beforehand. I just arrived carrying everything I owned in plastic bags on the handlebars of my bike. It only took three journeys. Fortunately, I was given permission to stay in the house with the other four women.

There were some mattresses going spare so I accepted one. I spent hours sitting in the room allocated to me on this mattress twiddling my hair and thinking. I slept sporadically. But every now and again, someone would call up from the kitchen to me and ask if I wanted to eat something. I said no, but then they would harass me to eat. In the end, I would come down and eat something just to keep them quiet.

It was very strange how time whizzed by. Most of the women in the squat were training to be carpenters or similar at a local training centre in Camden. This meant that they would leave early in the morning. I remember one of them saying to me with indignation, when returning at the end of the day, that I was in the exact same position that I was in when they left me in the morning. This was true but I just wished I could be left alone.

I had a strange all-consuming powerful headache. My thoughts felt like a big jumble of wires all mixed up in one concentrated area in the centre of my brain. The feeling would not go away. Each night I would try and work out the best way to commit suicide, so that people would leave me alone and that would solve everything but each morning I would be thoroughly disappointed with myself and my ineptitude that I had failed again to end my life. This went on for weeks. I tried once to ask for help. I said to one of the other women, 'I think I need to see a

Breakdown

therapist,' she just answered, 'Well, we all need to see therapists.'

I managed to get it together to go to Bristol and visit Marta. The knotted headaches in the top of my head were still bad and I told Marta that I thought I might have a brain tumour. She insisted on taking me to the hospital - the Bristol Royal Infirmary on the Monday, first thing.

The doctor asked me, 'Do you feel sick?'

'No,' I replied.

'Do you feel giddy?'

'Well, no,' I said, after thinking about it for a minute.

Have you vomited?

'No, not in ages' I said.

From this short set of questions, the doctor deduced that it was unlikely that I had a tumour and there was no need to do further tests. I wasn't convinced but it reassured Marta.

After I had left and returned to the squat a few days later, she sent me a lovely card. She wrote that if I felt ill and lost that I needed to get strong before leaning on another relationship, I needed to hang on in there and gradually my enthusiasm would return. She said that my security comes from being answerable to myself and that I was intelligent and strong. It was one hell of a card.

But I still couldn't motivate myself to do anything at all and bizarrely I was still having the driving instructor turn up outside Rebekah's flat each week for the driving lessons I had paid for. I went up to the driving school office in Tufnell Park to stop them and get a refund. I explained that I couldn't do any more lessons as I wasn't well. But they told me that refunds weren't possible as I had booked a block of lessons. They then asked me my new address and the instructor started turning up outside there instead. I gave in and had the final two lessons but I couldn't concentrate at all, made a mess of the driving and the instructor got very frustrated with me.

More weeks went by with me being useless and depressed. Then, unexpectedly, Rebekah came to visit one of the other women in the house. Immediately my motivation to do things returned. I was ecstatic to see her. I ran out to the shop to buy a pint of milk to ensure that

111

A New Man

there was enough milk for her tea.

I immediately cleaned myself up. I found out that she was going to the camp at the weekend. So, I got my stuff together to go. When I was there she came over in the evening and asked me why I was there. I didn't feel good at being at the camp at all but Rebekah had talked to me and that made me feel a hundred times better.

Gradually after a while, with the insistence of the other women in the squat getting me to eat and talk with them, I started to get better. I imposed a basic structure on myself. I wrote a list of things to do each day and awarded myself a tick in a box next to each task if I achieved it. The first task of the day was to get up. The second was to brush my teeth and third to get washed; fourth was to get dressed, fifth was to have breakfast. Sixth, wash up, etc. Doing this motivated me as I could chart my improvement.

I began living more normally and socialising with others, including demonstrating. I joined at the non-stop vigil against Apartheid outside the South African Embassy. I went to the 'Jobs for a change' festival.

I loved my bedroom. It was the first time in years that I had my own space that I could do what I wanted with. I painted it cornflower blue but it was bare, with only a mattress, a sleeping bag, my records and clothes in it. I phoned Marta and asked her to bring up everything I owned that she had kept with her since leaving York which she did reluctantly but it was a good feeling having everything I owned in one place again.

13

Lipstick Lesbian

The women I lived with in the squat were all training to be carpenters and the like at the Camden Training Centre. They suggested I should go along and see if there was something I would like to do. Manual trades didn't appeal much but design and printing did.

The careers advisor there suggested some courses at the London College of Printing so I wrote to the college to find out more and then applied. Following an interview, I was accepted onto a course – the B/TEC National Diploma in Business Studies - Printing Management option. I was very happy at this and looked forward to becoming a student.

I researched grants for the cost of the course but from what I'd now read it wasn't looking so positive. The course was £300 in fees alone for one year and I wasn't eligible for a grant. I had no idea as to how I would get that kind of money. Then I discovered that I could pay the fees in two instalments and that legally I could sign on whilst doing the course as the hours I studied didn't exceed the maximum allowed. I had just enough money left in my bank account to pay for the first instalment and so at least I could start the course.

In the house, I was the youngest member and also the only one in a relationship. I felt the odd one out. The others were mostly middle class, confident and good at cooking. There was a cooking rota and regular house meetings so I had to get my act together and provide food once a week. I was quite nervous about that although I could see it was fair. Rebekah helped me prepare a meal each week for five women and we were getting on well but then I ruined everything.

Rebekah held a dinner party. I was riding high on my newly found confidence as I was going to be a student and I was happy. Late in the evening after the guests left, Rebekah went to bed and there was

A New Man

only myself and Beth, Rebekah's lodger, left at the table. We were both extremely drunk. I looked up to Beth and was attracted to her. We went to bed together. I didn't remember how it happened even the very next day. But I didn't think about Rebekah, I just thought about myself. In the back of my head I thought Rebekah would never know so no harm would be done. But at the exact moment that I left Beth's room, carrying my clothes in my arms to go to Rebekah's room was the same moment Rebekah came out of her room to go to the kitchen and she saw me. The ending of the relationship was swift.

I was distraught for months and found the break-up difficult to accept. I tried to meet up with her. I'd go to her local pub, to the clubs we'd been to together, trying to find her. Sometimes I sat outside her house for hours. I became obsessional. I wrote her letters but never received a reply. I was so angry with myself for messing things up. After months of no contact, I began to think that wasn't any hope of us getting back together again and that the only way to get over Rebekah was to try and meet someone else. I put a personal ad to meet someone in the alternative Londoners magazine of the time, 'City Limits', and it turned out to be very easy.

I met Lucy, who was very attractive, not much taller than me with short dark hair and blue eyes. We got together nearly instantly. This relationship was based solely on sex. It worked well mostly because she could only cope with sex where we both kept most of our clothes on due to her own issues from family incest. Although she teased me for not being very butch it was, in essence, a butch-femme relationship. I kept my fantasies to myself, especially given she would have freaked out if she knew I was thinking I had a penis.

College started and I found studying very enjoyable. I now had an identity other than the ex-Greenham Common Woman one and I was a proud student. I even wore the Student ID card on my jacket lapel long after I'd left the building. The course stream I was on, printing and business studies, only had male teachers and I was for the most part the only female student. I'd gone from one extreme of spending 100% of my time with women to the other – spending most of my days with only boys and men. I didn't encounter problems. In fact, I preferred studying with boys, it was easier than with heterosexual women who I felt I had nothing in common with. In the evenings, I went out to lesbian bars where I felt I was amongst my own kind.

As the second part of the fees was needed in January I had to try and raise money somehow. I wrote to grant-making organisations, I visited some charities and organisations but I was continually rejected. I then decided to write to wealthy people and explain my situation hoping that they would feel some sympathy and feel like contributing a small amount. I looked up the names of people in the phone book who lived in wealthy areas and wrote to them.

This plan was not successful. I only managed to raise £50 from one generous family. It seemed as if the only option left would be to ask Colin. I wrote to him and explained the situation I was in and that in order to continue studying at college I needed money for the second instalment of fees. He wrote back and said it would be best if I visited him to discuss it all. This was not at all tempting. I had flashbacks to the farm, to the arguments, to the break up. I remembered when Marta had written to Colin's parents and told them he'd beaten her up. They had come up to the farm to try and sort things out.

His mother was talking to me whilst I sat beside her on the staircase with her next to me. I reluctantly listened to her drone on, having to put up with her excuses for him when I abruptly got up, ran downstairs, slammed the front door behind me and ran out. I started running out of the farm and past the gates. Colin came after me. He called out, 'Where are you going? You've got to tell me; I'm your father.'

Amazed at him saying this, which he hadn't done before, I shouted back at him, 'You're not my FUCKING father!'

He stopped in his tracks and I saw the shock in his face. I'd never sworn at him before. My breath felt ragged but I felt strong. He could feel the force of my anger and he backed off.

Being at the farm would bring back all these unpleasant memories. I wrote back and explained that I would find it too upsetting going back up to the farm. There was a long delay before his next letter. But when

A New Man

he did finally write, he said he had hoped that I would have healed those hurts and that the past was of small relevance and that he felt I was just trying to obtain money from him.

He got that right, of course; I was trying him out of desperation for money. Colin continued, he said he was planning to sell the farm, so it was possible that there might be some money left over. But he ended it by saying, he wouldn't give me any money unless I came to visit him at the farm up in Yorkshire.

Lucy hitchhiked up to York with me. When we got to the farm house that I had my hated teenage years in, I was gobsmacked as the house was transformed. It was now cared for; Colin had carried out home improvements such as installing French windows and the whole place had been properly decorated and looked smart.

This was upsetting. All that went through my mind was 'Why couldn't it have been a nice cared-for home when Marta and I lived there?' At dinner, we discussed the money situation. Colin's new lady-friend, as he called her, said that Marta was useless with money. I bit my lip and tried my hardest not to say anything. It was obviously a grossly inappropriate, insensitive thing for her to say.

That night Colin and his lady-friend made love very loudly. It was so ridiculously loud it was as if he was trying to make a point of just how good a lover he was. We were not impressed. The next day he gave me the amount I needed for the second instalment for the first year of the course and some extra money which I was grateful for but I was desperate to leave. Lucy and I went into York, and I showed her around the touristy parts. We went in to a pub and, unbelievably, Colin was there with his lady friend. So, we had to spend time with them. I had a bit to drink and I told him of my mini-breakdown and identity crisis. Colin showed a complete lack of interest and I kicked myself for telling him.

Back in London, I found that I was quarrelling a lot with Lucy. We didn't have a meaningful connection, we didn't even get on that well and when I next saw Rebekah I knew that I had to end it with Lucy.

Jane, my former school friend, who had now moved to London after also spending time at Greenham, was now coincidentally also living in my squat and she had left a note on the table that she would be going to Rackets. I was annoyed with myself for forgetting about the jazz nights on Wednesdays at the women's club 'Rackets' in Islington. So that was where Rebekah had been going out all this time, I said to myself.

I went along to Rackets the next chance I got and sure enough Rebekah was there. I was so pleased to have found her. Sharon, a friend of hers came up to me and told that I had to quit staring at her. I hadn't realised I'd been staring. It seemed harsh.

When it was time to leave the club, we spoke to each other outside the club. It was very emotional. Rebekah had a tear running down her cheek when we said goodbye to each other and I turned to walk to my bike. I had drunk more that night than ever before in one sitting – about 10 pints. I drank so much because I was nervous and I drank because I felt so bad that I wasn't with Rebekah anymore. I wanted her back.

At around 4am the next morning, I woke up under the lights of an x-ray machine at Bart's Hospital. The last memory I had until that point was the emotional parting and then walking up towards my bike. I don't remember unlocking or getting on to the bike, I certainly don't remember falling off or crashing. What an idiot I'd been.

I was woken up every half an hour and my reactions were tested to check for any brain damage. The amount of alcohol I had consumed meant that I didn't feel any pain and I enjoyed all the attention I got from the nurses. Fortunately, the X-ray didn't show any cracks in my skull but I looked terrible. One ear had swollen to nearly twice its size and to protect it, I had a bandage right the way around my head. I was covered in grazes with a bad gash on my forehead.

The next afternoon the hospital wanted to discharge me but they wouldn't let me leave until I had arranged someone to collect me. I phoned home, but everyone was busy. Then as a last resort, I phoned Lucy but she was busy too, signing on but thankfully her mum was able to pick me up.

When I went to the police station to collect my bike, they told me that they had found me in the gutter. I must have hit my head on the

A New Man

kerb. I'd unlocked the bike and I guess attempted to get on it and fallen. I happened to see Rebekah at the bus stop a few days later, she of course had no idea what had happened and was shocked to see me in the state I was in with bandages all around my head. After this chance meeting, we arranged to meet and talk. we had such a strong bond between us. I felt that our love was important so I ended it with Lucy and got back together with Rebekah.

By this time, I felt relatively comfortable about my lesbian identity. I had stopped worrying about my identification with the male body and supressed my feelings. In June, I marched on the Lesbian Strength March. These were held separately from the main gay Pride marches. In the early 1980s there were less than a thousand women on these. I felt raw and vulnerable being on the streets and shouting out that I was a lesbian to gawking onlookers. I agreed that lesbian visibility was important but at the same time I also disliked feeling on display and having to demonstrate about it and be stared at. At college, I also felt isolated.

I was offered a discretionary grant for the second year at college from ILEA (Inner London Education Authority), which I was immensely pleased about as this meant my fees would be paid and I'd even get a small maintenance grant. I would be able to complete the whole two-year course. Before restarting the second year at college, I moved to a squat in Kennington which was closer to the college at Elephant and Castle. This place suited me better, it was another women-only squat but with no rotas or house meetings. A room became available and Toni moved in too. Living in the squat meant that my outgoings were low and I cycled everywhere, at the end of the first term I even had some money left over.

The following July, I passed the course with a distinction. I had this honour with two boys in my year. I was incredibly proud of this and felt it made up for doing poorly at school. I had the choice of going on to do a degree in Business Studies full-time but I was specifically interested in printing so I decided to go on to the B/TEC Higher National Diploma in Printing and Business studies at the same college.

Lipstick Lesbian

When I got my first grant cheque that September for my new course I spent half of it on a brand-new road bike. Road biking and racing was my latest obsession and I even joined a proper racing club. To make up for this extravagance, I got a job in a supermarket and I accepted an offer of a bar job in a lesbian nightclub called 'Martina's.' The club night organisers chose the name after Martina Navratilova, the out lesbian tennis player and the club was hugely popular despite our night being on a Monday.

I had never actually worked behind a bar so I had to guess what was required for the most part but fortunately most women just wanted pints of beers so it wasn't too demanding. I enjoyed the work. I even adopted a bar-maid persona and started wearing lipstick and a black and gold shimmery top for my work. I wanted to look good, I didn't want to look dour and grey and of course no men were in the club so I didn't have to worry about attracting men's attention. I was complimented on my looks by the clientele in the bar. I experimented a bit and once wore a dress to the club though the shocked reaction (some women literally screamed when they saw me) was enough to make sure I never did that again. Anyway, I didn't like how wearing the dress made me feel.

Although I liked not appearing so butch, I definitely did not like male attention and the same went for any attention from butch women. In fact, I didn't want anyone to fancy me for wearing lipstick and looking more feminine. I was confused with it all. Women I fancied were mainly feminine, sexy, strong and independent women but I didn't know how to be a woman myself. I also didn't want to appear unattractive, which I thought men and butch women were in general. The option I felt most comfortable with was to be a lipstick lesbian.

I started being attracted to other women. I knew I could never make the same mistake again of being unfaithful. So, just two years after we got back together, I made the decision to end the relationship with Rebekah. She asked me to rethink it one last time. She said she feared this would be the last time. I swallowed hard and then said 'Yes, it is over.' This time it was for good.

A New Man

After the split, within a short space of time, things became unsettled and I lost my stability. The first year of the HND course was over apart from one more exam so it was the summer holiday period with correspondingly less structure in my life, which didn't help. Home life was deteriorating with a split amongst the women and I was unhappily stuck in the middle. Next, we were broken into and my precious new road bike was stolen from the house. To top it all a woman I slept with one night began stalking me, to the point of smashing a window in the house to get in to see me.

Then another event took place which took me over the edge.

14

Mania

'Lesbian Strength' was a separate Gay Pride organisation and in 1987, they held a huge party at 'The Fridge', a nightclub in Brixton. It drew lesbians from all over London. Many of us from the squats in Kennington, including one woman called Frankie, went to the event, which was about a 15-minute drive away. It was a good night and although most of had a few drinks none of us got particularly drunk. Afterwards, Kathy was going to drive some of us back in her van. I enjoyed being with her and I liked her a lot though it had already been established there was no chance of a relationship.

In a good mood, I got in the van and sat next to Kathy in the front passenger seat. But suddenly Frankie opened the front passenger door, grabbed me by my jacket, pulled me out of the car and dragged me along the road, causing the gravel on the road to scrape skin off my back. I was outraged.

In a flash of anger, I got up from the road onto my feet and punched her in her face. Frankie immediately hit me back and she continued to strike me again and again. I didn't hit her back though and then I fell to the ground and coiled up into a ball in the road expecting her to stop soon. Frankie then started kicking me hard. She was bigger and stronger than me. I kept thinking she had to stop soon as I was not returning her blows but she didn't, instead she continued to kick me again and again. I tried to protect my head with my hands and they instead got the brunt of her big boots.

Kathy and the other two women screamed at Frankie to stop but she was in a rage. It finally dawned on me that she had no intention to stop and that the only options available to me were to fight her back – I'd clearly lose and I had no desire to hit her again – or to try and run away as fast as I could. I chose the second option. I managed to scramble up

A New Man

and then I ran fast. She tried to run after me but she wasn't fit enough to catch me, this was one advantage I did have.

About a mile or two down Brixton road, Kathy drew up alongside in the van and picked me up to take me home, to my great relief.

'Are you okay?' Kathy asked.

'I think so, yeah, I just feel shaken up,' I replied. 'I can't believe what just happened.'

'Me, neither, there was no excuse for that behaviour whatsoever!' Kathy said.

My hand was swollen with a huge lump appearing, my head throbbed from the blows and I was shaken up. Frankie was not a close friend of mine, I didn't even know her that well. She was just someone I saw around because she'd started having a relationship with a woman in the squat I lived in. None of us had seen her act like this before.

Kathy dropped me off outside my front door before driving off to her own place. I opened it, ran downstairs into the kitchen and then the living room and called out for the others but there was no answer, I ran up to the top of the house, looking in all the bedrooms hoping someone else was around. But there wasn't anyone, I was alone in the house.

I retreated into my bedroom, shut the door and then sat on the edge of my bed, anxious for the others to get back as soon as possible. After what seemed like ages waiting for the others to return, I heard a loud banging on the main front door and shouting. It was Frankie. She had not had enough and wanted to hit me some more it seemed.

I was now stuck – trapped in the house alone and in a vulnerable position. I was terrified. Then I heard other voices, the others were arriving back. They then opened the door, and let her in as they didn't know what had happened.

All they could tell was that Frankie was really angry with me and they didn't know what was going on. I heard heavy footsteps coming up the stairway to my room.

My bedroom door was flung open and Frankie came in. She was just about to lunge after me to attack me again when Julie, a tall and strong Irish woman, a recent new resident, pulled her back forcefully. Frankie knew that with Julie there she couldn't hit me, she calmed down and then proceeded to talk to me sitting in the middle of my bed. I felt numb. I was huddled up, grasping my knees by the pillow end. I wanted her to go. I felt invaded having her in my bedroom, sitting on my bed.

She went on for ages going on about how she was working class saying that I didn't know her world. I didn't get her logic. I didn't want to continue to fight and I didn't see why I had to. In my mind, there was nothing wrong with getting away from the situation. She had more than made up for my one punch. I thought she should know when to stop. Julie stayed with us both until finally Frankie left me alone and went back to her own place.

I heard some years later that she thought I was a coward for running away. But what option did I have, if I didn't want to have a full-blown fight? It baffled me. I don't understand what caused her to continue to lay into me the way she did and why she didn't stop. What made her want to pull me out of the car? Jealousy? Because she thought I was presumptuous in sitting next to Kathy and that maybe she wanted to sit next to her instead. The only thing I can think of is that my punch must have triggered something from her past because she so was angry.

The next day I had the last exam of the year, but my body ached and my hand was very swollen and I felt fragile and shaky. I hadn't slept much either. The next two nights I drank a lot. I was physically trembling but I was determined not to let this event get to me. I cycled strong and fast down Brixton Road and said to myself that I would be alright.

Discussions started circling around in my head. Why did feminists claim that men were the only ones who were violent? Men were clearly more violent than women but women could be as well. I was also not good at controlling my anger and had been violent. Did that mean that I was more male then? But then I recalled hearing about the lesbians in Leeds having huge fights at benefit gigs and breaking chairs over each other. Were they lesbian feminists? Were they only anti-male violence?

A New Man

I just began thinking things through again and realising things were so much more complicated.

I wondered if perhaps Frankie was more male, like me inside. In my hyped-up state, I had so much to think about. But when I went round to her place to talk to her, she said it wasn't a good idea me being there and asked me to leave. My mind continued to spin.

One woman in the local squatting community, not a close friend but one I liked, could see that I was in a fragile, yet hyped-up state and stayed over in the same room to try and help me get to sleep but I just couldn't, so she ended up not getting any sleep either. I became severely insomniac during my unstructured summer holidays. I tried to visit people as I felt safer and saner with others around me but I couldn't rely on people's kindness and generosity forever.

The nights of no sleep continued. The women in the squat tried to get me to see a therapist. I visited a therapist and felt better, stable for a few hours. Being with her calmed me. Rebekah came over to see me too. It was good to see her and I calmed down for a bit.

But then I started to lose my grip on reality. Paradoxically, I started to feel confident. It was like a switch had been turned. I thought life wasn't bad, there were infinite possibilities. I should have a break and go on holiday, give myself a treat. I thought to myself 'Why not go to Switzerland first?', where I had such happy memories. I wanted to go but I wasn't together enough to organise tickets and transport my bike over there and organise somewhere to stay. That was all too much for me.

I then told everyone in the squat that I was definitely moving out and I started staying with friends, hoping I'd find somewhere to move to soon. I thought it would be easy to find somewhere else to live but it wasn't especially considering the state I was in.

I did however manage to get an appointment with an organisation for the homeless to try and get somewhere to live. I had no idea it would be this difficult and I had started to become desperate. To add to the pressure, friends were quite clear that I could only stay one or two nights at the most when staying over so I had to constantly move around.

The women at the squat now said they didn't want me back, even if I wanted to come back, due to the state I was in. They had had enough because I had been behaving very strangely. I don't remember much but I was told, for example, that I stripped off after having drunk a lot and had ran down the road naked and another time I had put up wooden boards in front of the front door to protect it from violent intruders.

At the interview with the homeless organisation, the woman sat me down on the worn sofa and then asked, 'Would you be fine sharing accommodation with women with alcohol or drugs problems?'

I shuddered, after the experience with Frankie, the thought of being around people being out of control did not appeal in the slightest.

'I'm sorry but I really don't feel safe around people like that,' I said, 'but I don't mind living anywhere, even Timbuktu.' I added, hoping I didn't appear too picky. But this was entirely the wrong thing to say. She frowned at me and said, 'Timbuktu is actually a very nice place.'

She then asked me, 'Have you got somewhere to stay temporarily, like on a friend's sofa?'

'Yes, I have some friends I could stay with,' I replied.

The trouble was, that just wasn't true at all. I just couldn't admit to myself or anyone else that I was truly homeless and that I didn't have anywhere to go. The interview didn't end well and I wasn't offered anywhere to stay.

I continued to cycle around, trying to visit people and find somewhere to stay. I'd repeat to myself that I'd be alright but then when I was cycling around, I began to think I was possessed, by the Witch 'Brenda', the woman I had against my better judgement got involved with at Greenham.

I thought her pre-prepared spell had finally started to work, set to this point in time. When I spoke, it was she who was speaking, her voice not mine. Her powers had reached me, laid dormant ready for this point. This really freaked me out. Try as I might, I could not shake her voice out of my body. I had pain in my shoulders and down my

A New Man

back from doing so much cycling and I had a horrible thought, that she could physically contact me and massage my back roughly, causing pain. Whilst cycling along I shouted at her out loud to leave me alone simultaneously aware that it was a bit strange for me to be shouting at myself.

Mania is clinically described as 'an abnormally severely elevated mood state characterized by such symptoms as inappropriate elation, grandiose notions, increased speed of speech, disconnected and racing thoughts, increased sexual desire, markedly increased energy and activity level, poor judgement, and inappropriate social behaviour.' Also, because mania creates high energy levels and a feeling that sleep is unnecessary, psychosis usually results from the lack of sleep.

My breakdown into a manic state came gradually, like a wavy line on a graph going deeper and below the line of sanity. Occasionally I would surface above the sanity line, then dip back down below again sometimes for days. So, I appeared to act perfectly rationally sometimes, or appear frustrated and at other times behave as if I was ultra-happy as if high on drugs. I never took any recreational drugs though.

Often people with manic psychosis think they have special powers and are chosen ones and I did think I was special. I was the potential saviour of the world. When I was feeling euphoric, I thought the world was wonderful and magical and that I could achieve anything if I put my mind to it. When I was in a more serious mood, then it was solely down to me to stop imminent nuclear war, which was a heavy responsibility.

One particular day, I was very distraught. The world was going to end as a result of a nuclear war and I was the only one who could prevent it. I had to get to Downing Street to speak to Margaret Thatcher before 7pm that night to plead with her not to use nuclear weapons. It was my responsibility to stop the nuclear attack. To achieve this, I gave away my newly bought brand-new racing bike to a very surprised young man on Kennington Road and hitched a lift with a lorry driver to North London, but I didn't get to Downing Street in time, I ended up instead in Islington.

Mania

I started catching taxis darting from one side of London to the other paying by cheque half believing there could still be a chance despite missed the deadline. Then there came a point when a taxi driver didn't accept a cheque, and he took me straight to Albany St police station.

I'd forgotten what I was doing and I couldn't explain to the police where I was coming from nor where I was going to because I didn't know myself. The black-taxi driver was kicking himself for giving me a lift. I was asked by the police to prove that I was who I said I was. Did I have a number of anyone who knew me? I gave them my mum's phone number. Although she wasn't in, she had an answering machine with her message saying her name. Because it gave some credence to me speaking some semblance of reality, they decided to let me go and sent the taxi driver on his way.

I remember thinking some months afterwards I hoped the taxi driver thought of me when the cheque cleared as he had assumed that the cheque would bounce. People who have manic episodes typically spend excessively and my finances were precarious at this point but I was only overdrawn by £500.

Trying to sort out my homelessness, I managed to get myself to a homeless centre in Tottenham Court Road and they told me they had organised for me to stay at a women's hostel opposite the Imperial War Museum in Lambeth.

When I arrived at the hostel, they said they knew nothing about me so I gave up and continued to be homeless. I had to sleep and rest somewhere. I found a place in someone's garden with shrubbery and a hedge adjoining the pavement so I slept there for a couple of nights hiding in the shrubbery. It was the summer, at least. In the blistering heat, I found myself on Clapham Common looking for an implement to commit suicide. I had concluded that I was utterly unsuccessful as a feminist primarily because I felt male and that I had no option but to do the honourable thing. I had no right to exist.

Whilst I was crawling around on the grass by the trees, I met a thin young man, who was friendly. He invited me back to his place. In this man's living room were stacks of pornographic magazines, literally stacks, piled up to waist height. We sat on the sofa and talked. He wanted me to have sex with him. I wanted to die. Eventually as I was getting fed up with his continual asking me to have sex which I was finding tiresome so I reluctantly agreed. We went into his bedroom. I said he should strip off first which he did. I was still not thinking about the prospect of sex.

Then suddenly I knew that I didn't want to be in his flat at all, never mind have sex and I ran to the front door. I got there before him but he tried to stop me escaping. My hand was on the door handle and his hand was on mine trying to stop me opening the door. I was stronger, thankfully, and I managed to turn the handle and run out and of course him being naked meant he couldn't run after me.

At some juncture during these episodes, when my manic state had subsided, Dad took me down to where he was living in Worthing. I felt awful having to tell him that I'd thrown away his birthday present to me, which I'd done in a hurry before catching the lift with the lorry in an attempt to reach Downing Street before 7pm. After a weekend with Dad, I stayed with Marta in Bristol. At Marta's I tried to get myself a bit more organised again and I phoned police stations and reported all the items I had lost.

Fortunately, I managed to locate my bag which contained my passport and other very important documents which I had left at the Oval House Theatre before heading off to Downing Street. I tried to sort myself out. I wrote many letters but also went out clubbing in gay bars and drank a lot, meeting new people. I got friendly with a woman, Jo, after a club night and we were caught snogging by the police in the shopping precinct in the centre of Bristol. It sticks out in my mind because they said, 'Oh look, two lesbians' and Jo said defiantly, 'I'm not a lesbian!' and then I said, 'I'm not either,' and then we both laughed at the picture of two women kissing but saying they weren't lesbians.

I wanted to get things organised, get stable, and find somewhere to stay. I was going to move to a tower block in East London with a friend but I am not sure what happened with this because I returned to London and soon after I was arrested by the police.

I had made my way to Downing Street with the intention of convincing Margaret Thatcher that nuclear weapons must not be used and that disarmament was imperative. When I was directly outside the entrance to number Ten Downing Street, I saw that there was a cordoned area of road works, I jumped into the hole that had been dug. I was half naked, I had taken my top off to show how serious I was, a sort of Amazonian peace warrior, I think. Immediately the police there hauled me out of the hole, I was arrested and taken to the Police station opposite. The psychiatrist later wrote in his report to my GP that I 'had some over-valued political ideas and paranoid delusions' and that I was 'from a culture of political crusade and protest and in many ways the behaviour was not unusual when considered in this light.' This was certainly true; another individual protest I had carried out involved doing U-turns on my bike outside Downing Street, imploring Margaret Thatcher to do a U-turn over her nuclear weapons policy.

In the police cell, I tried to communicate with people all over South London by bashing the plastic pillow on the wooden bed base in the cell as it made a very loud noise. I thought I could communicate with them. There was a small window in the cell which looked out over the Thames and beyond. I peered out and imagined that people could hear me all over South London. I did this for hours, bashing the plastic pillow. But I think this gave the impression to the police that I was in an extremely aggressive state.

When they opened the door some hours later, six large policemen pushed me to the floor and then lay on me whilst they handcuffed me. I could hardly breathe. I was then transported in a van. There was an uninterested police woman accompanying me in the back, despite me asking politely where we were going, she refused to tell me.

I was being taken to Tooting Bec mental hospital.

15

Mental Hospital

I woke up some hours later lying on a plastic mattress with a thirst like I had never experienced before. I could just make out a silent figure standing next to me with my eyes barely open. I seriously thought it was the devil and I was terrified but all I knew was that I needed water desperately, my throat was so sore.

I croaked, 'Water, please, have you got any water?'

But the figure walked out. Gradually I became brave enough to open my eyes fully and look around. I saw that I was in a padded room but the door had been left open. I was scared and confused. I didn't know where I was. I decided to try and get up.

I tried to stand up and walk but the doctors must had given me far too much of the incapacitating drug, Largactil, because I couldn't walk properly. I could barely put one foot in front of the other. I came out of my cell, staggering, and saw other people.

I opened my mouth to speak but then my tongue fell out of my mouth and I was unable to control it. I couldn't speak properly with my tongue hanging out. What was wrong with me? And where was I? I thought that it was me at fault.

A woman of about my age took to me to one side, laughing at me and said, 'Don't worry, it's the drugs making your tongue hang out, it'll wear off.' This was at least somewhat reassuring. I was grateful for her information.

Some hours later, I was ushered to sit down on a row of benches with tables and we were given food. This was intimidating and alarming. Instead of being confident and manically high, I was now the total opposite, a nervous wreck. I kept my head right down ensuring that my eyes did not meet anyone else's as I felt so fearful of people around me. My hands shook as I tried to bring the peas up to my mouth. It was

Mental Hospital

hard to eat and I still had little appetite.

I discovered I was in locked ward. I can only surmise that the police told the hospital I was violent. Why else would they have dosed me up as much as they did? I didn't know how long I would be incarcerated. On the ward people mostly just sat or walked around the ward in circles and continually asked others if they had a cigarette. An older smiling man gestured to me to follow him to the sleeping area, then he showed me his penis. I politely nodded and then retreated. This didn't particularly bother me, I just wondered why he did it. The woman of a similar age on the ward was in a manic state. She had a lot of energy and ran fast from one side of the ward to the other but she was friendly so I felt I had a soulmate.

A day later, on the TV which was bolted on to a wall high up where you couldn't reach, they showed the news of the Hungerford shootings, when a 27-year-old man went on a killing spree. I was very shocked by that and thought that maybe I had something to do with causing it.

Later when the Largactil prescription had been reduced, I was taken into an office with nurses and they told me my mum was on the phone.

'Hello Charlie, how are you? I thought you were lying in a gutter somewhere.' Marta said.

'How did you know? It's true, because I was in a big hole outside Downing Street.' I replied.

I hadn't spoken to Marta, for ages it seemed, yet suddenly I was able to speak to her. It was as if I'd forgotten about telephone technology and the ability to speak to someone when they're miles away. It felt like a magical experience to hear the voice of my mum, someone who cared. In my illness, I had forgotten about her.

A few days later I was moved into a more relaxed open ward, with no locks. I'll never forget a lovely Caribbean nurse who made me feel safe and cared for as she ran a bath for me. She showed me how to use a flannel to block the bath hole as there was no plug, all the while giving me dignity and privacy.

Now on the second floor in the open ward, I was able to see the hospital buildings properly. They gave an intimidating and depressing

A New Man

impression befitting of an asylum. The tall dark brown brick buildings had outside iron stair cases and covered walkways from one block to the next together with a massive iron fence. It reminded me of a Victorian prison.

I continued to have illogical thoughts. I believed all the vinyl records belonged to me in the recreational areas. And any nice-looking bikes and cars I saw through the window were mine as well. I thought they had been put there especially for my benefit, for me to use when I needed to. It's very difficult to describe this feeling, this state of mind, but it was one of optimism, of possibilities and it felt good.

Whilst I was in the open ward, Toni and Marta came to visit me. Marta was nervous of coming on her own and had asked Toni to accompany her. We played scrabble. When we played, all the words I placed in the game had meanings relating to mental health. I laughed and remarked that it was mysterious that I had the necessary tiles to do those words. I was immensely pleased they had come to see me.

Despite my serious psychotic episode, and continuing strange thoughts, I was discharged after only a week. It seemed the section I had been put under was only for a short period and I think because I hadn't exhibited any aggressive behaviour on the wards they thought I was well enough to be discharged but I most definitely wasn't. I walked out later that day with a black bin liner with some of my clothes (I guess Marta must have brought some underwear and stuff). Of course, I didn't have anywhere to go though, because I was homeless.

I headed for Toni's new flat (she had moved out of the squat around the same time I left) but I didn't even make it to the tube stop where she lived. Over the next few weeks or so I was arrested, sectioned and released a few times and taken to different psychiatric hospitals including the Maudsley Hospital and one in East Dulwich. A lot of the time, the police didn't know which hospital related to my post code (they used the post code of my former address) hence being sent to many different hospitals.

I remember some of the incidents that took place during the times I wasn't in hospital, like the time I was arrested outside Harrods for jumping into parked cars which had their sports roofs down, and attempting to drive them away as I felt such a strong sense of ownership - the amazing super posh cars had been left there for me deliberately, it was a great feeling.

On the converse side, I was picking up things that had been thrown away. A man on the street suggested to me that I shouldn't pick up rubbish from the ground. I saw rubbish differently. I think when you don't have much, these things start to appear to have value. You want to have something to cherish and to call your own. I had collected about a bag full, but after being told by this caring man on the street, that it wasn't such a good idea. I stopped it.

When not in police cells or hospitals, I tried to visit friends as much as possible but they were getting in shorter supply due to my strange and sometimes aggressive and violent behaviour. It turned out I smashed quite a few windows during this period. I stayed with one woman, an older, sensible friend who had had relationships with women and had also had breakdowns herself. She was kind and put me up one night. That night, I felt very sexual when I was lying on her bed next to her, then my body began behaving as if I had no control. It was bizarre and bewildering because my pelvis thrusted involuntarily even when I stood up. I was disturbed by this and was slightly hysterical, not knowing what was going on.

My friend didn't react and ignored me. Confused and frustrated, I went to the bathroom and I had the urge to bang my fist against the window. I smashed it unexpectedly and the glass cut deep into my arm. My friend came in, saw the blood all over the floor and bath and angrily shouted at me, 'You stupid bitch!' The female word 'bitch' made me wince but she called for a taxi and took me to hospital. I looked at the deep bleeding gash on my arm in the taxi, horrifically it looked like a vagina to me. This was an additional punishment I thought to myself. At the hospital, I was given a tetanus jab and my arm was stitched up when I'd stopped wandering around the corridors. I was sectioned again soon after.

16

B&B Accommodation & Council Flat

Eventually I stabilised on medication at hospital and then got somewhere to stay. I bumped into someone who worked at the Citizens Advice Bureau one day and he was certain that as I had recently been released from psychiatric hospital and was homeless, the local council had a legal duty to help me. I had no shoes and was walking the streets in just socks; my feet had blisters. (I think the shoelaces taken from me at police stations were not returned and then the shoes came off easily and I lost them.) My mum had come up to help - somehow, she found me. Maybe she collected me from a hospital or a police station. We stayed with Lucy's mum for a few days, who was very helpful, and Marta bought me a pair of trainers.

With the CAB advice in mind, we went to the Lambeth Law Centre and what we had been told was confirmed, that the council was obliged to house me. After the interview, the solicitor gave me a compliment slip with their contact details.

The next day after going back to Lucy's mums in Walthamstow we went to join the queue at the Lambeth council homeless service. Although we got there at 9am sharp, we weren't seen until the end of the day. The man at the counter asked why I couldn't stay with my mum. Marta replied that I was going back to college and moving to Bristol would mean I'd have to give up the printing management course I was half way through. He wasn't impressed by this and persisted with his argument that I had somewhere to stay, though my mum didn't have a spare bedroom or even a sofa for me to sleep on.

Then I remembered the comp slip from Lambeth Law Centre and I pressed it up against the glass window separating us, showing him the details. I said, 'These people told me to see you.' Immediately his attitude changed, he went to see his manager, came back after a few

B&B Accommodation & Council Flat

minutes and said, 'Yes, we will help you with accommodation.'

My mum was very pleased but I was not at all reassured because I had heard about people being stuck in horrible B&Bs for years and years and I dreaded the prospect. I had been phoning places up, trying unsuccessfully to rent a room, but I still wasn't well enough nor stable enough. I was given vouchers and the address of a B&B in Pimlico; despite my worries, I had no money for a deposit so I had to go along with it. I was pleased to be given somewhere to stay and a roof over my head, but I was petrified that I would be in a B&B for years.

The B&B was called Hotel Diana and had a landlord called 'Mr Beg.' I arrived there late that evening with my mum. I think she was finally able to breathe a sigh of relief. Before saying goodbye, she warned me that I needed to continue to take the medication, that it was vitally important to stay well. I had such a low opinion of myself; it was demeaning to me, that I had to take medication just to be stable like everyone else.

My room in the B&B was a tiny box room on the ground floor, which had very old fashioned decor with dark wallpaper and dark maroon curtains. There was one small bed, a small old fashioned TV, a wardrobe and chest of drawers but no desk. All the electrical sockets were the two-pin foreign old type so you couldn't use your own electrical equipment.

The breakfast was the stingiest breakfast imaginable: Two triangles of toast- one poached egg but the butter to spread on the toast was a measly thin 20mm x 20mm square. No matter how thinly I spread it I couldn't make it cover the two triangles of toast. Sometimes ants crawled along the dining room table. There were no other residents there, save a mother and two children but they couldn't speak English so I didn't have any company.

There was nowhere to shower. I had to wash using the basin in the toilet outside of my room. I could have a bath but had to ask special permission to use Mr Beg's own bath. As you can imagine, I wasn't that keen. But the absolute worst thing about living at the B&B was that I had to be in every night by 10pm and have the register signed

A New Man

each day. Mr Beg explained that if a Lambeth council housing officer visited and I wasn't there, then I would lose my right to future accommodation and be chucked out, (because if I was elsewhere this supposedly meant that I had somewhere to stay) which consequently meant a severe restriction on my life. Mr Beg took pity on me and he was at least understanding about the unfairness of this so that he offered to sign to say I was there when I went to see my mum at Christmas.

I was desperately lonely, and I felt low and insecure from the comedown from the high I had experienced being manic. Marta, and Dad came to visit me once separately, right at the beginning of my moving in but I didn't see many other people as I'd lost most of my friends due to my previous disturbing and sometimes aggressive manic behaviour.

Gradually I got used to being at the B&B and started to feel more comfortable there. I intended to go back to college but on my first day back it was evident this was not going to work as I sweated and shook physically from the medication. I also found the amount of college work I'd be doing intimidating. There was nothing for it but to ask for a year out and I thought maybe I could work instead for the year. I asked for references from college. I thought it would be helpful if I could try and get a job in the printing industry whilst I took a year off and I managed to obtain an interview. I had to try and sort out something suitable to wear and to be smart and this meant getting my ironing board. Dad had come up to London and helped me moved my stuff from the squat and into the council storage. Other people's areas at the storage centre had beds, wardrobes, cookers and fridges and the like. My little allotted square was just a pitiful table, a chair, a mattress and a few bags of clothes & books plus the ironing board I now needed. I got the iron and ironing board out of storage and carried it on the bus back to the B&B.

Mr Beg then refused me permission to use my own iron and ironing board. I was annoyed and frustrated by this. He said I could only use his iron in his room and he even insisted on charging me 35p per item ironed for the electricity, which I thought was extremely petty.

After all that preparation, I didn't get the job. Perhaps the interview-

B&B Accommodation & Council Flat

er thought I was selling myself short for asking for a low wage as he had asked me what I think I should earn. Maybe he wasn't interested in hiring a young woman; given the considerable prejudice against women in the printing industry, I wouldn't have been surprised. Or maybe I still looked shaky and unconfident, I am not sure, but it was disappointing.

To keep myself occupied and to help me talk to other human beings during the day, I enrolled for some adult classes at the local school opposite the B&B. I chose Spanish, Typing, Maths and Karate. I wrote out a timetable for me to do the work and decided to try and be positive about learning until I got a job.

Only a couple of weeks later, I saw a job in the job centre I was eligible for: Administrative Assistant in the Department of the Environment as only three 'O' levels were required. As I had the distinction in the BTEC national diploma in Business Studies, I thought this should suffice. I was offered an interview.

I paid my £1:05 to use the electricity to iron my interview clothes, went along and I was offered the job. I discovered years later, when I obtained my medical file, that they had contacted my GP to check that I would be okay as I had revealed that I had had a nervous breakdown on the form. Luckily for me, my GP said I should be fine.

The admin job at the Department of the Environment meant finally I had some regular income coming in so I cleared the debt that I had amassed when unwell. At the B&B there weren't any cooking facilities available for the residents and having an off licence opposite meant I ended up buying bottles of lager and chocolate far too often. I put weight on and got spotty. But now I had a job I could go to the work cafe and afford cooked food.

I had to give up the day classes but I could at least continue with the evening typing course. At the class, when we were typing out our CVs, I wrote my address and the woman next to me in the class suggested I drop any reference to the B&B for prospective employers, which was embarrassing. She pointed out that having a B&B for an address would reveal that I was homeless and or without a stable base. However, I

A New Man

learned to touch type at this class, a skill which later proved very useful.

Regrettably, the job at the Department of the Environment turned out to be pretty monotonous as I had very little to do. My tasks comprised of ordering stationery and organising and distributing press cuttings, but that was about it. Also, it was for a project I didn't even agree with: the privatisation of water. However, having the job meant that my overdraft cleared and I felt more like a member of society. I enjoyed talking to people at work and felt accepted because although we didn't have much in common, the other colleagues were friendly and we got on okay. This improved my well-being because as I said I didn't have many friends left.

I had a friend called Paul who was one of these few friends and he was very accommodating. I'd met him through Gina. I'd go up to his flat in Islington regularly and we'd hang out listening to music. Paul had an unusual background, he went to school in Uruguay, Tanzania and England and University in California, before settling in London. He was empathetic about my breakdown and I stayed in his room and relaxed often, not worrying about having to talk.

Whilst I was at the B&B I heard my dad had had a nervous breakdown; this, at least, is how his former partner had put it. I instinctively thought he had attempted suicide. It turned out this was correct. Like me, he had also gone to a bad place. He had effectively been constructively dismissed and he believed he had lost his new relationship too. He was living in a flat on his own. One day he cut his wrists and took an overdose. Maurice, a long-term friend of his from school, then phoned Dad to remind him they were due to go out for a drink and was wondering why he hadn't shown up. So, Dad answered the phone, didn't want to let his old friend down and so went out had a drink with him having wrapped his wrists with bandages. The mixture of the alcohol with the tablets Dad had taken made him vomit, and so expel the lethal concoction. I am forever grateful to Maurice because his actions saved my Dad.

Poor Dad, I felt for him. I knew what it was like to feel your life is not

worth living anymore and think that people would be better off without you. We had both taken a big tumble at the same time. Dad however managed to bounce back from this quite quickly though, without
medication or therapy and he soldiered on.

I started driving lessons again, something I'd been meaning to do
since abandoning the driving lessons at Greenham Common and then
at Tufnell park when I wasn't well. I found the perfect instructor, a
confidence-inspiring woman.

Gradually I got better and I even started seeing someone, a self-
assured woman I met in a nightclub but I wasn't quite up to sex. That
was a step too far, too scary and still a psychological minefield and I
was unable to do anything more intimate than kissing. But it was nice
to have someone to spend time with and be close to even though it fiz-
zled out after a couple of months as she lost interest in me.

I asked the doctor at outpatients if I could come off the lithium as I
was convinced it was making me feel very low. She refused to sanction
this but she said some people do come off it and never have another
manic episode again. I contacted a Lesbian and Gay organisation that
provided counselling and was told someone would contact me two
weeks later but for some reason no one ever did and I didn't chase it up.
I was allocated a new psychiatrist who I didn't warm to in the slightest as he was distant and standoffish. He said I would be very likely to
have another manic episode if I came off the lithium abruptly and that
I'd be back in hospital within six months. I didn't want to hear this. I
ignored his advice and stopped taking it as it was making my world so
grey and miserable.

The Department of Environment admin position was so boring
that despite finding out in February that with the qualifications I had I
could be in a higher, better paid position, I decided to leave and work
as a cycle courier. I got a position with a successful courier company – called 'On Yer Bike'. They had so many clients over a small geo-
graphical area that I could pick up more than one package, take it to
an address and then pick up two more packages at that address. I was
rarely 'empty' – I got a tremendous amount of satisfaction from the

A New Man

job, I liked the people and I felt like I was achieving something useful.

I returned from work one day to a major upheaval. I was told by a strange woman I hadn't seen before at the B&B that Mr Beg had had a heart attack, was in hospital and that I had to leave the B&B immediately. Shocked by this terrible news, I was then jolted into action, into auto-pilot mode. I used the B&B phone and called the Lambeth Council emergency line. They said they would call me back. I waited anxiously. Half an hour later they called and said there would be a taxi arriving in an hour to take me somewhere else and they instructed me to pack my belongings.

I ran out to the grocery shop nearby, bought some bin liners and put all my stuff in them. I also had my ironing board to take. The other family went off in a different taxi. I explained to them the best I could what was happening. My taxi then took me to a B&B in King's Cross which I had been told would be expecting me.

No such luck. When we arrived, the people at the B&B said they had no knowledge of my arrival at all but the driver didn't care, he had done his bit and he just dumped all my stuff on the pavement. The front door was shut. I was left standing with all my belongings in the black bin liner bags on the pavement in King's Cross, late at night with nowhere to go, I felt abandoned yet again. I rang the bell on the door of the B&B hoping to speak to someone about the situation. The B&B manager decided to let me stay for the night and said he would ask Lambeth Council about my situation in the morning. It did thankfully get sorted out the next day.

This B&B turned out to be far superior to the place in Pimlico. It had white walls and blue curtains and there was a lively, friendly young crowd staying there. You could also have cornflakes in the morning and toast. Such luxury. Breakfast was an enjoyable experience and people were upbeat. The only downside was that the TVs were coin operated. You'd be watching something good on telly and then without warning the screen would suddenly go black, which was annoying. It was common for residents to be asking others for 50p pieces at all hours.

After six months of living in a B&B, the housing team at Lambeth

B&B Accommodation & Council Flat

Council called me to inform me they had somewhere for me to live. I was ecstatic. I had had visions of being in a B&B for years, this was much quicker than I had thought. The housing team said I had three choices but not at the same time: if I turned down the first then I couldn't change my mind on seeing the second place. I accepted the first choice, I knew I wouldn't want to be in the position of turning one place down only to be offered one I desired less.

I contacted the solicitor at Lambeth Law centre and thanked her for all her help as she had been persistently writing letters to Lambeth Council for me, after it had been confirmed by my GP that I had been severely mentally ill requiring hospitalisation.

I collected the keys and went off to see the place in Brixton. It was a ground floor flat in a Victoria conversion. It looked okay, a bit dark inside but when I unlocked the door to my flat inside the communal corridor I was a bit disappointed. It was obvious that the council had just evicted a family, and very recently. There were personal items lying around, toys, clothes in the washing machine, even food had been left on the sideboard. It was upsetting to think I'd partly been responsible for their eviction.

The flat was also in dire need of repair. Floor boards were missing, there were big holes in the walls, the bathroom window was completely rotten and there was mould in the kitchen. I made a list of all the repairs needed and reported them. I also informed the council of all the items of furniture, the sofa, bed, wardrobe etc., which had also been left behind and that there were two enormous old TVs and a bath in the garden. Three months later, I was told all the repair works had been done and that I could move in. I turned up to view again, excited, but was dismayed to discover that only the furniture which was in good condition had been removed, probably because it was sellable.

The TVs and the bath were still in the garden and there were many repair jobs outstanding but I was just so desperate to leave the B&B that I could wait no longer. I accepted the flat and signed the forms. The rent was only £17 a week. It might have been in a terrible state but it was affordable and more to the point, it was now my place, my very

A New Man

own place. I was supremely grateful to Lambeth Council for providing me with a home and therefore some stability.

The next day I moved in. I chucked out all the old food, toys and clothes. I opened a cupboard door and was sad to discover a box of birthday cards and wedding cards left behind by the family. I waited a few months, in case they returned to collect them, but then these also had to be chucked, as realistically I had no way of contacting the people they belonged to.

There was no central heating in the flat. I had one gas fire in the front room, in winter months later I would sit down by the fire burning my legs, trying to get warm. I bought a cheap convector heater which worked well in the bedroom and I got dressed straddled right over it trying to get warm. The bathroom was at the extreme end of the flat past a very badly designed kitchen which regularly suffered from a leaking washing machine above. I returned one day from a night out to discover the bathroom ceiling in the bath. I also discovered Victorian conversions don't tend to work very well in terms of noise, insulation and layout.

Despite this, it was such a privilege to have my own place. I felt like I'd be there forever. When it was later suggested I bought it under the 'Right to Buy' scheme, I considered it, but I felt that the council had helped me when I desperately needed it and consequently I wanted it to stay council property for the next person.

I had complete control over the bills and everything down to the atmosphere within the flat which was a liberating feeling. Life started to improve after moving in. I felt positive and confirmed with college that I would return to finish the HND in Printing Management that September. Although I was still on medication, it was only lithium now so I didn't have to suffer from the 'largactil shuffle' or twitchiness which had prevented me from returning the previous year.

Notification of my driving test day arrived in the post, set for May 24th. I was given permission to take the morning off work. It went well, when the instructor turned to me at the end and said, 'That was a lovely smooth drive; You've passed,' tears welled up in my eyes; I was

B&B Accommodation & Council Flat

overjoyed. I had passed first time.

I stopped off at a phone box in Clerkenwell in the afternoon, after I'd dropped a parcel off and phoned Marta to give her the good news. She sang 'congratulations' to me. I was so happy. It felt like more than an average achievement for me because I had learnt to drive whilst I was at rock-bottom, homeless and living in a B&B with barely any friends. Now I had somewhere to live, a job and had a driving licence. At the age of twenty-two, things were looking up.

17

Unable to Marry

Before going back to college in September, for the final year, I thought I should have a holiday. I wondered about the possibility of going to Switzerland again. I wrote to Sarina to see if she'd be up for having me stay with her. We had continued to write to each other over the years and we were on friendly terms. She agreed. The first night on arriving back in Switzerland, Sarina suggested we went to a lesbian film show. I wasn't particularly keen as I wouldn't understand much but I decided to go along.

I don't have any memory of the films at all but a large group of us went for a meal after the films and that was very memorable. At the restaurant, we sat at a large round table. Opposite me was a stunningly attractive woman. She had short shiny blonde hair and blue/green eyes and light olive skin. She was very flirtatious and kept giving me sideways glances whilst smiling. I smiled back. Later that evening, when leaving she introduced herself as Claudia, handed her number to both me and Sarina and invited us both for a meal with her and another friend, Helen. Very forward, I thought, which I liked. Sarina could tell I was keen to meet her again.

We arrived outside Claudia's flat about 20 minutes early. I didn't want to ring the bell until it was the time of our appointment but Sarina brushed aside my need to follow polite protocol and my desire not to appear too keen.

Claudia was polite and friendly. We entered her flat. It was immaculate, tidy and modern with a habitat-style sofa and chairs and a small bookshelf and a TV, nothing else apart from the dining table. She asked us to sit at the table. On the table were little bowls of gherkins, boiled salad potatoes, crisps, salad and placed in the middle was an electric grill to heat the traditional Swiss Raclette cheese. It was a sim-

144

ple but effective traditional Swiss meal.

Claudia sat opposite me. Whilst Sarina and Helen were intellectualising about politics in Zurich, I was completely distracted by Claudia. She was smiling mischievously. After the meal when we were relaxing, she told me about her recent birthday party, the fact that she was now single and also how she was clear she didn't want to have children. At that point, I felt the same. She phoned two days later and said asked if we both wanted to go to a party on the lakeside on Saturday? I obviously wanted to and Sarina decided to go too. At the party, Claudia and I were able to get a moment to ourselves in a secluded spot by the Zurich lakeside and we kissed. I stayed over with her that night. I then had a puncture and so used the excuse to spend the next day with Claudia.

I ended up spending much of the rest of the holiday with Claudia. My relationship with Sarina had finished long ago but it was still inappropriate of me to start a new relationship right in front of her. My only excuse was my youth and inexperience. Sarina was gracious and said that I couldn't help falling in love, but I did feel a bit guilty as I didn't spend much time with her before I returned to London.

Claudia was thirty and I was now twenty-three. Although she was less politically involved, she exuded stability, was open-minded, intelligent and incredibly good looking. Claudia said she'd only had relationships with men up to that point but that she was interested in me. I was flattered. The relationship continued after I had to go back to London.

On my next visit over, Claudia wanted me to use a penis prosthetic. With her encouragement, I was interested to try it out too. We went to a sex shop and obtained something we thought would be suitable. This was so very different from lesbian sex I'd had up until then and when we had sex I loved it, though I felt it was daring. There were further plane trips for both of us, between Zurich and London. There were long expensive phone calls. I made strenuous efforts to improve my German and I started lessons.

It was heart-wrenching saying goodbye at airports and I pined for her when I was in London. I longed for the day we could be properly together. She seemed perfect and I was in love. Claudia wrote numer-

A New Man

ous letters and cards to me declaring her love for me too. Her words were so overwhelming I found it difficult to believe her. She sometimes spoke so fast, she'd miss off the word 'Ich' (which is 'I') and she'd just say 'liebe dich' fast and repeatedly which is 'love you'. Gradually I started to let her words sink in and I believed her.

The problem we began to realise was that it was going to be extremely difficult for us to be together because we were both women, on the face of it, and consequently our relationship was not officially recognised. Coming from different countries meant we couldn't live together. Switzerland was not in the EU either (it didn't agree to free movement until 1999).

I suppose there might have been a small possibility of me managing to obtain a job and therefore a visa in Switzerland but it felt extremely unlikely. I was studying printing management but working in the Swiss printing industry would be tricky as a trainee manager because so much was different, including different paper sizes and different print terminology. I had already written to the Swiss Printing trade organisation for information and the response wasn't encouraging but the overriding problem was that because we were both women we couldn't marry each other and therefore we couldn't stay together either in Switzerland or in the UK.

It seemed the only way we could live in the same country was if Claudia married an English man to stay in England or conversely if I married a Swiss man to stay in Switzerland. We would have to convince the authorities that the marriage was bona fide. It was a deeply unpleasant predicament to find ourselves in. I didn't want to pretend I was in love with a man.

Eventually, though we decided it had to be me because my preference to live in Switzerland was stronger than Claudia's desire to move to England. I advertised for a 'gay husband' but in the Swiss gay community this wasn't easy. The men in Zurich gay centre openly laughed at me when I explained what the ad was for when I asked to pin it up on the notice board. Marriage for convenience was much more common in the UK. In the UK gay press, a long list of adverts from people

Above: Unwell
Below: B&B in Pimlico

Above: Having break with Marta
Below: My Council flat!

Above: On a night out
Below: The four of us together – Dad, Me, Marta and Justina for Dad's 60th Birthday

Above left: Relaxed and casual
Above right: Uncomfortable in female business attire
Below: Lipstick lesbian

Above: Happy, post-chest surgery
Below: Getting ready for Pride March with Fraser and Jay

Above left: Trying a beard
Above right: First suit
Below: Eight years on testosterone, 45 years old in 2010

As I am today – 2017
Photo by Nick Figgis

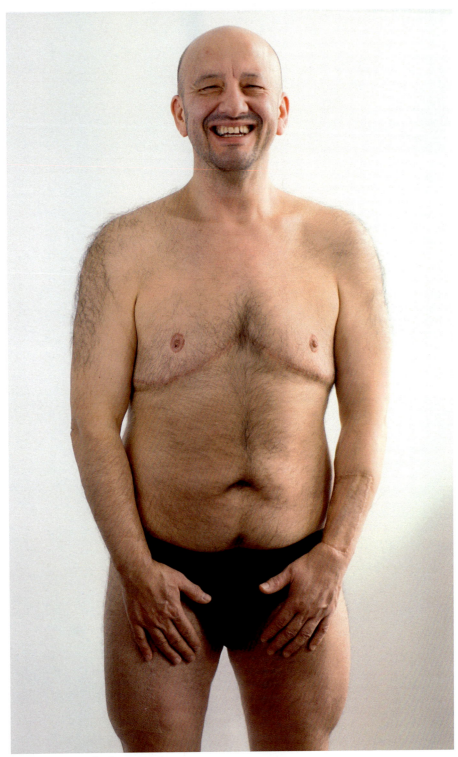

Happy in my new body

Unable to Marry

desperate to live with their partners and to come to 'a mutually beneficial arrangement' was a regular feature. I know of a lesbian American and British couple who got married to gay male counterparts.

I was due to stay in Switzerland for a whole month over the Christmas period, but my Swiss future partner and dreams of a better life in Switzerland came to an abrupt and unexpected end. Unusually, when I phoned her just before leaving London, Claudia said she wouldn't meet me at the airport and that she would prefer to meet me at the Zurich rail station instead. She didn't give a reason other than being tired and when I arrived late at night, she appeared distant and uninterested. The next day, not being able to deal with the uncomfortable tension I decided to try and have a proper talk with her.

'What's wrong? Have I done something to upset you?' I asked.

Claudia then said, in a cold, dispassionate voice, 'I don't love you anymore.'

'Why? What has happened, what's changed?' I quickly asked, feeling a heavy doom-laden sinking feeling in my stomach.

But Claudia couldn't say why or she didn't want to. I was bewildered and devastated. That night I cried for hours sobbing into the pillows. How could this happen? When we were so in love, I didn't understand at all. She hugged me and apologised for causing me such pain.

I said I really shouldn't stay in her bed and I moved to the living room and slept on the sofa. She thought I was overreacting but it made perfect sense to me. I was so shocked and upset, my instinct was to return immediately to England. I phoned Marta, she thought I should stay and to try and resolve things, also money was a problem as I would have to buy another plane ticket. I only had enough money to live on until the next term's cheque so I didn't have enough for another plane ticket. I didn't want to leave Claudia but she didn't want me anymore. So, what could – what should – I do?

When Claudia returned from work and I hadn't left, she was relieved and it appeared that she'd changed her mind. I felt she still loved me. I went out and bought her truffles and champagne, we slept together, had sex and hugged each other tight.

A New Man

The next day though she reverted to being cold and distant again so I went back to the front room sofa. I tried to be helpful and useful, I did tons of cleaning, did all the washing up every day and did the shopping thinking stupidly that this would make her feel better towards me.

Then Claudia got flu and I helped her again in every way possible but it was futile. It was over and I was not wanted. I had made the wrong decision not to leave right away.

Initially she had said I could stay with her until the date of my flight back but then she changed her mind. She asked me to do some shopping for her then that afternoon when I'd come back with the shopping, she abruptly came out of her bedroom into the living room and said,

'I want you to go.'

'But can't you tell me why?' I responded, 'Surely I have a right to know why you don't love me anymore!'

'You don't have any rights, you STUPID woman!' She shouted at me with such venom.

I was so upset at just being discarded when I was going to give up my whole life to move to Switzerland so that I could be with her that I lost control and I hit her. She gasped in shock, I felt terrible and wanted to comfort her so I hugged her.

She phoned her mum and I could work out that her mum suggested calling the police. I wasn't going to take any chances, I rushed out without even taking my stuff. There was only one place I could go to in Zurich at a moment's notice and that was at my ex, Sarina's. I phoned her up outside from a phone box. She told me to come over.

Half an hour after I had arrived at Sarina's, a taxi arrived with my suitcase. Claudia had despatched me properly and decisively. I felt completely taken for a ride. I had believed her when she had declared on so many occasions she was completely in love with me. I could not work out what had gone wrong. I felt extremely low. I felt wretched and bad about hitting Claudia.

That night I went to a gay theatre bar and I started talking to a man there. He said he was bisexual. I could see where things were leading and I went along with it. I even paid for the taxi to his place. I wanted to

148

be punished for my behaviour and to do something destructive. I very nearly had sex with him but he had an unusually large penis so it didn't happen. When he was in the shower, I just let myself out quietly and then walked all the way back to the Zurich city centre through the still quiet night feeling I was worthless and life was so bloody miserable.

I phoned up Claudia the next day and apologised. She wanted her T-shirt back which I still had, so I went to her house and pushed it through the letter box as she'd asked. During another phone call a few days afterwards, she told me she'd decided to give me some money and thought that was fair, given that she had left me in a difficult predicament.

I had by then decided to stay on in Switzerland, though, until my flight back in January and the money went quickly over the remaining time left, despite the fact that I also got paid for one night's work helping a mutual friend hang up pieces of art for an exhibition.

Staying at Sarina's for such a long time, I tried to avoid being under her feet, but she became resentful as we weren't getting on. I began to wish I had gone back. After an argument over a pint of milk, (I'd been unable to find a shop open to get a pint of milk ready for her when she returned from spending a few days away) I decided after thinking about it all night that it would be better all round, if I just left, so I wrote her a note explaining and left her flat the next morning, there were only a few more nights left before my flight back.

Switzerland in December was cold, many degrees below zero. I spent a lot of time hanging around in cafes making a cup of coffee last ages or sitting outside on a bench. I manged to sort somewhere to stay for a couple of nights through meeting someone friendly at a nightclub and then a mutual friend also helped out the last two nights I was in Zurich. I was so looking forward to flying back home to England.

When I landed at Gatwick, a full month after being in Switzerland, I wanted to kiss the ground. I was numb but so pleased to be back. I didn't mind the rubbish lying around, or the late, slow buses; it was home and so different from the sterile, super-efficient Switzerland. It was good to be around familiar surroundings again and to speak and

A New Man

hear English.

I rang Claudia a few months later and a man answered the phone, so I wondered whether she had started a relationship with a man and had been unable to tell me. I'll never know why she had had such a change of heart. Perhaps the problems of us being from different countries was just such an insurmountable bureaucratic ordeal just to be able to be together, and then there was the language barrier, we mostly spoke in German but I still had a lot to learn. I think it all became too much but I wish she'd told me before I'd left London.

This experience made me extremely envious of the right to marriage and angry at the injustice of not having equal legal rights. When Denmark became the first country in the world in 1989 to permit equal marriage, I was immensely pleased and I became hopeful that the rest of the world would soon follow and give everyone equal rights. I had to try and forget Claudia and turn my attention towards my college work. I started to get good grades which was uplifting but I thought about her often and what could have been if only I had been male.

I next had to start looking for a job as the HND in Printing Management was due to finish so I went to Oxford street and bought two skirt suits in preparation for interviews. One was a stylish blue suit with a shiny two-tone blue/green lining, the other was simpler, a cheaper basic black one.

A major downside of entering the world of work was that I was going to have to wear skirts and wear tights and - the horror of it - shave my legs again. This was going to be difficult fitting in the female world of work but necessary. I would've much preferred to wear trouser suits but in the 1980s these were not considered appropriate for women at work and especially not in the traditional world of printing. I expressed my frustration with having to wear skirts with a lesbian office worker friend of mine, but to my surprise she didn't mind at all and thought I was being precious.

Despite feeling depressed about the relationship ending with Claudia, I finally re-focussed and immersed myself into college work. As I had obtained good grades it was easy to get job interviews. But I found

Unable to Marry

them tough. It was going to be a hard change finally leaving full-time study and getting a proper job.

One interviewer asking me about my experience at Greenham Common, she was worried about my capacity to be discreet and she mentioned Government contracts. I wasn't offered the position. I realised putting my time at Greenham Common on my CV could be a hindrance and a distraction. So, I removed Greenham from my CV. My time in prison wasn't a problem at all, however. This was because the offences were categorised as civil offences, so surprisingly despite being in prison I didn't have to reveal them.

I went to the interviews wearing my skirt suit, court shoes and tights. The court shoes were agony, because I had no experience of wearing heels whatsoever, even though they were only 1.5 inches high. I probably looked smart but I didn't feel comfortable physically or psychologically and that was bound to show. It was very stressful trying to look the part and I couldn't even walk upright properly. I tried putting paid relief pads in. My feet got blisters. Why was this pain and hassle necessary? I didn't get it. I looked around at other women in the offices, wondering how they did it. They certainly looked more comfortable, maybe they had just got used to it over the years. The thought of having to wear shoes like that forever was not appealing; I hoped I'd only have to wear outfits like that to get the job.

At my third interview, I was offered a job as a production manager and I accepted it. I started my new job a week later but the printing management office proved an unfamiliar environment though and the other people in the office were very competitive.

Every morning a young woman, the secretary, made us all tea and she brought the cups right over to our desks, which made me uncomfortable. I questioned this but I was told categorically that this was standard, the subtext being that as a manager I should accept being served by the secretary as part of the role.

Disappointingly, the company turned out to be print farmers. Print farmers are companies that don't own any print machines or do any of the work themselves – they instead sub-contract all the work out. I

A New Man

had been given the job on false pretences. At the interview, the director had showed me around the print room of another company positioned below our offices. Although they clearly had an agreement, he had implied that the companies were one.

Consequently, my job entailed print purchasing only and not print management as I had to deal with other printing companies which was completely different to organising things in your own company. I wasn't introduced to any of the printers – just given a book of print company names and addresses and left to get on with it. I wasn't comfortable with this at all.

Three days later the course results were published and pinned up on the notice board at college. I had done well on the course- with 3 distinctions and 5 merits. I was really pleased. I didn't sleep at all that night. The next night I managed to sleep for a few hours but again the following night again I didn't sleep. My mind began to race.

The following Monday at work, despite my efforts, I was having difficulties in getting a job printed. I became stressed. There was no help or support in the company and I didn't know what to do. I became slightly paranoid about other people in the small firm and I started obsessing about the work. On the Friday evening I needed to leave a note for the director but then I started to think about what colour note I should leave and about the symbolism of colour. I left a pink note in the end, thinking about gay liberation (pink being the gay colour as this was the colour of the triangles gay prisoners had to wear in the Nazi concentration camps). I think I even wrote something about liberation on the note as well. I was losing my grip on reality again. I had an interview lined up that evening for a Business Studies evening degree course at South Bank University but I didn't make it.

The next day I resigned.

18

Relapse

The psychiatrist had said I would have a relapse and another episode of mania if I came off the lithium abruptly. I hadn't believed him but he was right, it just took six months longer than he had predicted.

After yet another night of no sleep following my resignation, there was a knock on the door, it was workmen from the council. They finally came and collected the two TVs and bath from the garden. It was comical that they'd finally come, a whole year after I moved in. I appeared normal and held the doors open for them as they moved the items out through of the flat but a few hours later I was arrested by Brixton police.

I had prepared a picnic on the road outside my house, a picnic full of blue crockery, as blue was the colour branding of the Conservative Party. I'd also put up barricades using bins in the road to stop the traffic. I was expecting Mrs Thatcher to come and sit down at the picnic and discuss the future of Britain with me. It was urgent as she seemed intent on destroying British industry with her narrow monetarist free-market policies. Most of my college lecturers were very worried about this too. I had come back into the flat to collect more blue items when I saw two police officers by my window.

A neighbour must have called the police. They stood right up next to the glass of my bay windows and tried to peer through my net curtains. I thought I'd better open the front door to them. On opening the door, two police men and a police woman barged in. I can't remember the conversation properly but they were rougher than they normally were to me. I think this was because despite my efforts to appear 'normal' I ended up having a conversation about sexuality and I told them I was only interested in women and therefore only the police woman. This wasn't received well.

A New Man

I was shoved onto my sofa, and a knee was dug deep into my back. I cried out. They put handcuffs on me and marched me out of my flat and roughly put me into the police van. The duty solicitor I saw later, at Camberwell magistrates court cells expressed concern at the extent of the bruises on my wrists and hands.

When I was in the dock, the magistrate asked me some questions. I don't recall what was said but the funny thing is that the magistrate took pity on me and he ordered that I be given £10 out of the police charity fund. The police weren't amused with this at all, but I was really chuffed. On my release from the Camberwell cells, with the tenner I immediately went bought myself cheeseburger and fries and caught the bus back to Brixton.

Later I visited Paul and his new girlfriend Ingrid up near Balls Pond Road in Islington. When I was there I got very wound up in an argument about communism and I removed all my clothes, I think I was trying to re-ground myself and get back to basics as it were. They eventually called the police which I don't blame them for in the slightest. I would have done the same in their situation.

The police took me off their hands but despite my friends asking me to be taken to psychiatric hospital to be looked after they just dumped me in King's Cross, which was a well-known area for sex workers to solicit.

I had put my clothes back on before being taken away and I was wearing black satin-look trousers, though it's hard to believe I looked good. I was barely there for five minutes before a middle-aged man stopped his car and asked if I'd like to go back with him. He seemed friendly enough so I did. It didn't occur to me that he would want to have sex with me. He took me up to his flat. He was not especially well off judging by his possessions and furniture. He asked me what I wanted to drink and I was given a cup of coffee. I saw he had some music by Suzi Quatro and we talked a bit about her and he played some of her music.

I thought he seemed alright but then he disappeared out of the room and came back in with just a dressing gown. He sat opposite me and his

Relapse

gown slipped and revealed his large, though un-erect, penis. I didn't react at all though and he realised his mistake in thinking I was a sex worker. I think he could tell I wasn't well and he offered to drive me to the nearest tube station, Shepherds Bush, so that I get back home.

On the way there though, he suddenly turned to me and said, 'Show us your tits then!' which obviously, I refused to do. I opened the door in indignation and threatened to jump out but he said I was being stupid. I had to agree and I shut the door. He then gave me £2 for the tube fare and we said goodbye. Whilst it was a potentially dangerous situation, I didn't feel in any danger. He hadn't tried to be physically close to me nor had he pressurised me and he'd even given me a lift to the tube.

On another occasion, when I must have explained I was hungry, I was given lots of chicken for free in a fried chicken shop on Brixton road, and then the owner gestured to me to go through a door which led to the rear of the shop. There at the back was a small bedroom, where his son was waiting. His son offered me money. I realised what he expected and I wasn't happy with the assumption. I argued with him and threw his money at him and escaped out the back door. I didn't feel under any physical threat again though, it was just the assumption that I objected to. I suppose he thought that as I was short of money I wouldn't say no to sex but it would've taken a lot for me to be in a position of wanting to have sex with a man willingly whether money was involved or not.

My lack of interest in having sex with men extended to more amicable meetings. During one period when I was feeling better, I met a young homeless man on the streets of Brixton who I liked a lot. We had both been picking up dog ends to smoke and started chatting. I befriended him and took him home. He was sweet and quite vulnerable in some ways as he couldn't read. I gave him a bath, some food and cut his hair for him but he also badgered me more than once to have sex with him and I flatly refused.

From 5th August until 20th September 1989 I was in and out of many police stations and psychiatric hospitals. Sometimes I escaped hospital because I valued my freedom greatly. But I'd often end up back

155

A New Man

in hospital through my actions. I would be improving and relatively stable and then I'd just go and do something spontaneously wild. I visited Gina's parents in North London. On my way back to Brixton, I decided that I would continue cycling past Brixton and cycle on to Switzerland. I made it half way to Dover.

It had become very dark, I didn't have any lights and I was hungry. At a road-side chip shop, I sold my bike cheaply, so I could hitch a ride more easily and buy some food. Later I regretted that - it was a good bike. At one point, I became frustrated with not getting a lift and sitting where the road split in two, I played dare devil with the cars, thinking I was invincible. Luckily, I was picked up by a friendly easy-going couple with a big van and two big dogs and they took me all the way to Dover.

It was late when I arrived at Dover and I had to make my way to the passenger bridge towards the ferry. The problem then was that although I had my passport with me, I discovered I was just a bit short of the money for the foot passenger fare onto the ferry. This was a big blow.

I decided to pretend that I couldn't speak English to try and get on to the ferry. I was taken to the transport police offices and was questioned all night. Very early the next morning a police officer then decided to get rid of me and he put me in the police car drove up and down the sea front before deciding to dump me right by the beach. His uncaring attitude annoyed me. I had no money or means to go anywhere.

I said, half-pretending, that I was going to swim the channel and started removing my clothes. He took this seriously though, and then arrested me, presumably for my own protection. I was taken to Dover Police station and kept in the police cell overnight. I felt strangely at home in the cell. I'd been in quite a few over the past month in police stations across London. I desperately wanted a cigarette but had to beg the police to give me one. I did get given a cigarette but it was one of my own which they'd confiscated earlier. They wouldn't let me smoke in peace on my own in the cell though, they said they had to watch me smoke it, something about to make sure I didn't do something stupid, which completely ruined the experience.

Relapse

The next day, I was convinced that I had somehow managed to produce some sperm and when three doctors came into my cell to ascertain my mental health, I wanted to show the sperm to them on the bed. They ignored me. After confirmation of mental illness, I was then taken to a psychiatric hospital in in Ashford, Kent.

After a week in this hospital, the nurses told me I would be given a ride all the way back to my home to London. I was pleased by this news but it turned out they weren't telling the truth. I was transported in an ambulance, which felt peculiar, then they didn't take me home, instead they took me straight back to South London Hospital.

I felt humiliated and furious at this deception. When I was brought in to the hospital, I threw some plates on the floor in the dining room. I was quickly carried to the lift, had my trousers pulled down, then five male nurses sat on top of me whilst I was injected in my bum. I shouted at them, 'Get off me, please!' I felt I was being assaulted.

I was heavily drugged and put on the locked wing of the hospital. It was similar to prison except more claustrophobic. There were just four small bedrooms, exactly like prison cells. The wing had a miniscule dining room with an orange plastic table and chairs for four, bolted to the floor and one other tiny room with just enough space for one armchair, a TV and an exercise bike. The other people on the ward, all men, were heavily drugged too, so there was no hope of a decent conversation.

Marta and Dad both came to visit me at different times when I was in the locked wing. Perhaps this was because they knew I'd be there as I couldn't escape. Marta brought some large posters of forests and streams with her and stuck them on the wall of my room, which cheered me up.

Some other friends visited me: Kristin, the school friend from York who I'd kept in contact with for years, Rebekah and Kathy. I was deeply touched. When Kathy visited, she spent ages rolling up loads of cigarettes for me, which was very handy because the drugs I had been given meant that my hands shook too much to roll my own.

Having my own flat, a stable base meant that I didn't become as

A New Man

severely ill as I had the first time. The psychiatric hospital was close to where my flat was and they let me go back to check up on it sometimes and doing that re-stabilised me. I kept it clean and tidy ready for my return. Also, I wasn't as frightened the second time, having experienced mania before.

Weeks later and I was still in hospital though I was much improved. This time in hospital I had at least made some friends. I got close to one nice woman though I was a bit disturbed by a swastika tattoo on her hand. I met a bloke called Trigger who was a visitor to another patient. He was constantly being sent to prison because he could never afford road tax and insurance; all he ever seemed to want was a car. He treated me like a mate and we got on well. I was ready to leave the hospital by now and enjoying spending time with others I'd met there. There was also Steve, a long-haired guitarist who reminded me of 70s-rock stars. However, he wasn't able to manage living on his own and was impressed by me managing to cook a meal for us both. He had sporadic periods at the psychiatric hospital but didn't seem that unwell to me.

I wanted to leave and had to convince the doctors that I had sufficiently recovered which was harder than you'd think. What worked in my favour was that I had started applying for jobs. I phoned up a printing company whilst I was in the hospital and lied that I was in hospital for a bad ankle in order to explain the background hospital noises and I got an interview.

The doctors on the panel were impressed by this at the assessment for my suitability for release and I was discharged on September 20th. I was looking forward to leaving, I'd had enough. Fortunately, I got the job. This was a trainee print estimating job in the screen printing company nearby in Brixton Hill, very low paid but at least relevant to my training.

When I arrived back home, waiting on my doormat was a nasty surprise. I opened the official-looking brown envelope, it was a letter warning me of eviction. As I had been ill I hadn't been working or been able to sign on, so obviously, my rent had not been paid and I was now

Relapse

in serious arrears, not really through my own fault. After frantic phone calls to the housing officer an arrangement was made whereby I would be paying back a little bit more each month towards the debt. At least now I had a job to be able to pay back the debt.

I had to take the lithium every day. The psychiatrists, Marta and everyone, it seemed, told me I had to, that it was vital to keep me stable, to prevent another episode. I was determined not to have another relapse ever again. Having manic episodes was just too destructive. So, I wasn't going to refuse, the trouble now, was that life was extremely monotonous and grey. Some of my low mood might have been the natural swing back from being so high but I was convinced the lithium also was a major cause of making life so dull and dreary, so depressing and pointless.

I had a flat and a job yet everything seemed lifeless. The job was okay but not especially interesting or rewarding and as I said, very low paid. I hadn't made any friends; all the other workers were either a lot older than me or lived very heterosexual lives that I could be no part of.

To try and re-gain some enthusiasm for life I started going to tap dancing classes every Monday evening but every day was the same, week in, week out, the tap dancing class was the one highlight of the week which felt pathetic. Feeling life was completely pointless, I put up a noose to hang myself with in my hallway. I wasn't sure if it was strong enough but I stood on a stool, put my head in the noose and then stopped for a moment and then the seriousness of the situation forced me to focus.

I thought about what it would be like afterwards. A nothingness, but a completely different nothingness. Although life was very grey and didn't seem worth living, I could see there really would be absolutely nothing after death. I would miss all the small things in life, that I enjoyed, like a cup of tea, or the beautiful view of the sky. All these things would be gone forever for me if I ended it. So, I took the noose down.

At the next out-patient's appointment, I explained to my psychiatrist what had happened. I even cried in front of him.

A New Man

'It's really difficult to kill yourself; you're more likely to end up being paralysed instead,' he said, 'And if you did manage it, which is unlikely, the world would be a worse place without you.'

I felt a bit better after he said that and when he offered me anti-depressant tablets, I accepted them especially as he assured me that I wouldn't need to be on them for longer than six months. I did not want to have to rely on yet another drug.

After the noose incident, I met up with Rebekah who was keen for me to see a therapist. Without much money, I couldn't afford it, I thought, but I managed to find a therapist in Brixton who charged me only £5 a session. Having a weekly consultation helped me get through the week.

Gradually life brightened up over the next couple of years. I got a better paid job over near Wembley, bought my first new car, a Datsun Cherry which had an entirely blue interior, even the steering wheel, which I loved. I went on holiday to Berlin. I joined my very active local Labour Party in Brixton, and became quite involved, helping with canvassing and enjoying the discussions at the meetings.

I also got myself an all-black kitten from an alcoholic woman I'd befriended on the street when I'd been unwell. It took me over two hours to catch him from the garden hut he was living in and put him in a box.

I named him 'Schatzeli'. This is a Swiss term of endearment- similar to 'darling' or 'sweetheart'. Claudia used to call me 'Mis Schatzeli' meaning 'My sweetheart'. He was lovely and kept me going. He was to become a companion of mine for over eighteen years.

After four years of no further manic episodes, the psychiatrist agreed in July that I could come off the lithium, and this time it was a managed, supervised slow withdrawal. I was warned to keep an eye on my moods and make sure I did not become too euphoric or worked up about things. I was officially discharged from outpatients after twelve months of not being on any medication in 1994 and five years after my second hospitalisation for mania.

I moved back to Kilburn to be closer to my new job. This was

Relapse

through a mutual council exchange to a flat on a modern council estate with a balcony and central heating. A change and a fresh start was just what I needed.

19

Split Identities

Sitting in the therapy room with my new lesbian feminist therapist in East Finchley, I told her that I lived a double life. In my work life, I said I was known as a conscientious worker, working amongst nearly all men but that I never felt comfortable. I explained that as soon as I got home, I changed out of my female work clothes immediately and re-adopted my dyke identity.

In my own time and outside of work I lived almost exclusively, apart from my friend Paul, amongst other lesbians. I only went to lesbian nightclubs. I was in a lesbian football club, being a lesbian was my core identity. The only time I spent with men was at work or in the pubs in Kilburn when I'd go and stand alongside them in the busy pubs watching Liverpool play.

I explained to my therapist my continued difficulties in relationships as most women wanted to relate to me sexually as a woman. I found this insurmountable.

After I moved to Kilburn, I had a brief relationship with a woman called Stephanie and when I was with her I experienced a degree of sexual liberation. Stephanie had been out with men and women and crucially she was open-minded about sex. At the Ace of Clubs, a long standing lesbian night in Piccadilly, I put my hand on her thigh and I could feel that she was wearing stockings. I cried because it felt so liberating for this to be acceptable.

The relationship developed and sometimes we had fun dressing up and role-playing. For example, I would be the older boss at work and she would be the new secretary or I would be the young inexperienced client and she, the mature sex worker. This was more exciting compared to my understanding of lesbian feminist sex which appeared to be so constricted. Make-up, which even I enjoyed wearing sometimes, was still frowned upon by many. Sex with men was definitely looked down on, so bisexuals had a difficult time, and many women were beginning to rebel against this type of stifling and oppressive feminism. Rules were starting to be broken, penetration was no longer considered patriarchal and sex toys became more popular (though dildos weren't penis-like in the main and were usually bright coloured such as blue or purple). A women's sex shop opened in Shoreditch.

For Stephanie's birthday, I offered to do something especially nice for her, at her request. She asked me to do a strip tease for her and wear a mini-skirt. I tried to do this as best I could, but I couldn't fulfil her wishes convincingly and I disliked doing it intensely.

She objected to me continually being 'the man'. I felt guilty as I didn't want to change things. I let her penetrate me once, as I felt I should, to be fair and equal, but of course it did nothing for me and she found she didn't enjoy doing it to me either. 'You're just too butch for words.' She declared.

In the next relationship, I tried harder to be accommodating. My new lover was quite masculine in bed (though she didn't appear masculine) and our relationship was more akin to a gay men's sexual relationship - vaginal penetration was out of the question for both us.

I heard about a drag king contest. I decided to enter thinking that I had a reasonable chance of winning. I thought up a whole new persona in preparation for the questions on stage. Where I lived, what kind of job I did etc. Before I went on stage I swapped tips with others for the best way to show a shaved face applying brown eye shadow over my cheeks. I wore brown trousers and a business-like shirt. I thought I looked very male, but, the event wasn't at all as I had imagined.

I was participating in all sincerity thinking this would be a competition on who appeared male the most convincingly, but this wasn't the case at all. The contest was about entertaining the crowd instead. I felt humiliated because the woman who won didn't even appear male and was just very good at making the audience laugh. Looking back, it was another obvious indicator, the fact I was upset that my masculinity hadn't been taken seriously.

A New Man

Then I met Carol and with her I could immerse myself fully into my male persona in a more heterosexual relationship, which I much preferred. Though of course, this was all unspoken; the secret of being a heterosexual male was in my head. It was when I was with Carol that I had my epiphany.

I recounted to my therapist that I had looked round and seen her purple nails on my shoulder and felt so turned on that I was with a heterosexual woman. She asked me, 'So do you think heterosexual women are more erotic than lesbians then?'

I laughed heartily at this.

'No, of course not,' I replied.

At the time, I wasn't able to verbalise that it was the validation that I was a heterosexual man which is what turned me on.

I needed to sort out my sexual identity, my inner conflict with gender, my relationship problems and my aggressive behaviour which had manifested itself once or twice in some of my relationships. Sometimes I wondered if I should be in a relationship at all and I dreaded being severely mentally ill again. For all these reasons, I had been seeing a lesbian and feminist psychotherapist.

I was now thirty-two. Eight years had now passed since I was manically ill and hospitalised and I was determined to remain free of all medication and to do everything possible to avoid another relapse. The trouble was that I continued to struggle over my body, and my relationships. I was frustrated. I felt disconnected from the body I had to live in.

On another level, I also found sexist comments more unpleasant than other women seemed to. Some women objected when I complained. I asked a supplier on the phone to stop calling me 'Darling.' But a female colleague said I was being the unreasonable one and that I had been rude. I wanted to be called 'Mate' instead. There are degrees of sexism but with me the slightest thing used to make my blood boil.

I despised it when a shopkeeper or barman would call me 'sweetheart' or 'love'. Other immense irritations were being patronised by salesmen when going to car mechanics or cycle shops - you were just

Split Identities

always treated like you knew nothing. And my pet hate was continually being told to smile and to be expected to be sexually attractive in so many situations. Cycling as a woman also meant you got a lot of sexual and sexist comments which really got to me. Of course, most women find this behaviour unbearable especially unwarranted inappropriate sexual comments. However, it seemed to me that most women did like more general complimentary comments, but I didn't want any man to give me a compliment on my appearance.

A manager once proclaimed, 'Men write, women type,' implying men were the original thinkers and that it was the woman's role to type out men's words. In one company, it was expected I make the tea for everyone, all of whom were men. I decided that I would make tea only once a day for everyone (to avoid feeling guilty) and I rigidly stuck to this. However, when all our desks were being changed around, the boss said until I'd made everyone a cup of tea, I wouldn't be told where I'd be sitting. I was livid and I walked out.

I found it difficult to be around men; older men tended to be more sexist and unpleasant and with younger men I was acutely envious. I was envious of their flat chests, their deep voices, their genitals, their clothes; I was envious of their masculinity. I wanted to be seen not as a potential partner by men but as one of them. But even in women's circles, I didn't stand out as particularly male.

Many lesbians didn't consider me butch and I didn't feel very comfortable being a masculine woman either. I said to my therapist, 'I'd much rather be a feminine man than a masculine woman.'

'What's the difference?' She replied, which surprised me. I considered there to be a huge difference and I knew which one I preferred.

When I carried out activities which were traditionally seen as male activities, such as football, (football was considered exclusively male when I was young) I put huge pressure on myself- that I had to do well. I felt that I should be of a high standard because I saw myself as more male and therefore more experienced in playing football. The reality of the situation was that I was average compared with most of the female footballers on the women's team I had joined. I gave up football after a

A New Man

couple of years as I felt under too much pressure to perform well and just wasn't enjoying it as much. I changed my focus to squash, which I started playing more regularly. I put in an advert for a 'North London Dyke to play squash with' in the Pink Paper, a gay publication, found someone friendly and we were an even match. We played together every week for years.

A catalyst to the beginning of the resolution to my gender conflict was when my two separate lives (my female work persona and my dyke persona) came together when I started work at the print worker's co-operative, Calverts.

At Calverts, it wasn't necessary to hide being a dyke, as people were open to that and in fact I discovered there were already lesbians working in the co-op. I stopped wearing skirts, as the work place was much more relaxed and I stopped trying to fit into the conventional feminine world at work. But in this new work environment, I could no longer keep two separate identities. I was now one whole person with one name, Charlie. This forced me to look at who I really was and to stop playing roles. I then met someone who had been involved with a lesbian who was a trans woman. This got me thinking again and all the thoughts and feelings came rushing back about wanting to have a man's body.

The door in my mind opened wide again. It had been three years since waking up that day with Carol and having that major epiphany that I just should have been born male. I had been supressing it hard since that day. (Although clearly it had surfaced before, such as when I was David, when I was a teenager and when I left Greenham, but I was unable to define it then or process it.) Now those thoughts and feelings were back and were stronger than ever. This time, though, I thought far deeper about everything. I understood that this was why I hated and envied men so much and why I was so angry. Being transsexual explained why I hated having the body I did. The reason for little things like why I would insist on always having bubble bath when I was in the bath so that I didn't have to look at my body, was now obvious.

It was upsetting looking back and remembering the pain and dis-

Split Identities

comfort of always not fitting in, not being yourself and being uncomfortable in your body and presence. I cried and cried, thinking back to my time as being treated as one of the boys when I was young. I liked being around boys a lot then, I remembered with nostalgia. It was so sad that I had kicked boys, men, out of my life for all these years. I found it difficult sleeping and I became quite wobbly. My therapist said I could call her whenever I felt the need to recognising the fragile state I was in, and I did call her on a few occasions either in absolute frustration or overwhelming grief.

I thought back to when I was a child, when I was growing up. I grieved for the years that could have been if only I'd been born male. I would never be a teenage boy, I would never be as tall as I would have been if I'd had testosterone in my system earlier. My first experiences with girlfriends would have been so much better. I may not have been spurned. I would have liked my own body. I may have even married and had children.

I had repressed my childhood dream of being a boy – I had called myself David. What had happened to David? I cried my eyes out. I thought over and over about all the misunderstandings and problems I had had as an adult trying to be comfortable in myself as a woman. I had an ambivalent relationship towards masculine, butch women. I saw similarities between myself and them but - and this might seem difficult to comprehend - I didn't think I was masculine enough to be a butch woman.

When I wasn't grieving for the lost past or feeling frustrated about what I should do, then I was thinking about the differences between men and women. It was so utterly exhausting... remembering and thinking about gender continually, thinking about appearance, about clothes, hair, how your moved your body, how you walked, your hands, the tone of your voice and how others presented themselves to the world. I looked at men a lot more and how they behaved.

I startled someone on a trans internet forum when I said that trans women didn't need to get handbags as very few women had handbags. No, that wasn't the case at all, the answer came back to me, 'You've

A New Man

been living in a parallel universe!' and then I saw that it was indeed true, that most women carried handbags. This was possibly another result of living in a lesbian sub-culture.

I rang the Samaritans at four in the morning needing to talk to someone about how horrible it was coming to the realisation that I was male whilst being at Greenham Common. No wonder it had been a shock, no wonder I'd had a crisis of identity, a breakdown.

Of course, I was male. Of course, this meant I was transsexual. But whether I could go through with transitioning was the big question. I discussed the problem with my therapist. She tried to accommodate me but I couldn't help noticing that she didn't hold heterosexual men in high regard, in one session she said in a disapproving tone, 'Do you really want to be a heterosexual man?'

I went along to an FTM London meeting (FTM refers to Female to Male, a slightly out of date term now, for a Trans man). The meeting was held upstairs in a gay bar in King's Cross. I walked up the stairs feeling quite nervous. Once in the small packed room I found the meeting very challenging. I couldn't help thinking that I was in a room full of short men with beards and I felt distinctly uncomfortable.

In the sub discussion group, I found myself in, two men insisted to me that they were men and always had been. They didn't seem to acknowledge their previous experience as being treated as female, which I found odd. Of course, I accepted they felt they were male all these years but I also couldn't help thinking that if people had treated them as female in the past, their behaviour must have been affected to some degree. Even though they may have been uncomfortable, they would have been referred to with a female name and forced in many instances to take on a female role. If there had been a female masculinity group at that time like there are now, maybe I would have been able to explore my masculinity more as a woman. The FTM group was too much of a leap for me at the time.

As the weeks and months wore on, I worried about the implications of physically transitioning and became overwhelmed at the prospect of going through all the changes brought on by hormones and surgery.

Split Identities

This was going to be hard and would require serious major adjustments and re-evaluations for me, my colleagues, my family and in fact everyone connected to me. What a massive undertaking it would be. I simply wasn't sure I was up to it.

I went once more to one of the FTM London meetings and this time I bumped into an old friend, David. I had met David in the courier firm I worked for in the late 80s. I'd heard through the lesbian grapevine he had transitioned so it was great to see him. We went out for a drink together and had a thorough discussion. He could see I was in a mental turmoil about it all and he encouraged me to see past all the murkiness and politics. He repeated back to me what I said to him. It was obvious that I'd be happier as a man. While I was with him, I couldn't help noticing that I felt supremely jealous of his flat chest and deep masculine voice.

Whilst still lingering in limbo land I made a decision I was 100% comfortable with. I would change my name legally to 'Charlie'. It was relatively straightforward. I had a statement typed up and then I had to read it in front a solicitor at a cost of £5 (officially called, 'swearing my statutory declaration') I was enthusiastic and excited about my name now being official. My old name said female. 'Charlie' was much more male but not exclusively. Once I had done this I felt a large part of me had been relieved of the pressure. A middle-class bloke at work didn't approve; he was bit of stickler for correct English and he said it was a nickname for Charles, which was the 'correct' name but I took comfort in the fact that Charlie was an official name and that it was by then a much more popular name for boys than Charles. But I was still 'Ms' Kiss. I was beginning to think that it was as far as I'd go though. It was all just too much to transition fully. I'd try and struggle on in the body I had – hormonally and physically as a woman, again.

Soon afterwards I met another lesbian, Katie, at a birthday party. She was slim, taller than me and of a similar age. Like me, she had left home at sixteen and experienced her later teenage years in the lesbian separatist community. We hit it off very well and could talk about all sorts of things – politics and life in general. She had a working-class

A New Man

background, was laid back and I was comfortable around her, we'd joke about a lot. I explained my position early on, that I was male identified. Happily, she didn't see this as a problem. Our relationship was successful sexually as she had a relaxed and liberal attitude and didn't want me to do anything I felt uncomfortable with and I felt under no pressure to be female in bed. Despite this, though, occasionally the transsexual feelings would still surface, the two times, I casually mentioned my desire to get my breasts cut off I got short shrift. I felt I dare not broach the subject of transitioning.

We were together for two years before I made the firm and final decision to transition. This happened after I watched a ground-breaking TV documentary called 'Make me a Man,' which featured the lives of some young people who had decided to transition to male. Watching these much younger people and their determination to transition to male was inspiring and put me to shame.

I knew then, I just had to go for it. I had to pursue my childhood dream. As Stephen Whittle, a pioneer and long-time campaigner for trans rights, wrote in a self-help book: 'There comes a point where you have to take a leap and trust'. It was time for me to do that.

But I had to tell Katie of my decision and both of us knew that it had to be the end of the relationship as Katie was a lesbian. We had returned from a trip to Berlin and barely finished unpacking when I told her.

'I've decided, I'm going to do it, I'm going to start taking hormones and start transitioning to male,' I said.

'You better leave, and right now then.' Katie said angrily.

I hurriedly gathered my stuff. I felt my stomach churn. As soon as I was outside and down the road on my bike I called Rebekah.

Crying uncontrollably, I told Rebekah what had happened. Even though it was fully expected, it still hurt to be ejected from her life so quickly and decisively. Katie was in shock, I was rejecting her as I was not going to be a lesbian anymore and I had decided to become a man without even properly forewarning her.

20

Becoming a 'New Man'

I had decided to start the process. I was on my own now and this was a journey that I had to sort out. I went back to the FTM London support group and started going regularly, feeling much more comfortable with the trans men and 'starters' there. I now felt that I was one of them.

The monthly meetings became important and I looked forward to them with great anticipation. I would enjoy thinking about what I would wear. I loved wearing men's clothes. I no longer had to pretend I liked blouses. I could wear shirts and choose absolutely anything to wear from the men's section. I often chose clothes from the men's section before anyway but had felt awkward and I was careful not to choose anything too masculine. I was always compromising. Now I could be totally free in my desire. The menswear shops were like treasure caves to me. I wanted to buy so much and enjoy the clothes. I'd been disparaging to my lover, with whom I'd felt we had more of a gay men's relationship, who wore men's underpants, but now I wanted to buy loads of them for myself.

I stopped wearing eyeliner. I had found it a very useful and easy female indicator in the past but now it was no longer needed, although this was a tiny regret I had at the time as I had developed a liking for it. Kristin, said I could still wear it as many men did, but I just thought it wasn't the right time whilst I was going to transition. I put my labrys silver chain in a box. This symbol of lesbian strength, a present from Rebekah years ago, had been a handy subtle indicator to other lesbians that I was one, but it wasn't going to be needed ever again.

I found it extremely helpful being at the FTM London meetings as I could work out how I felt being treated as male in a safe place. Here everyone no matter how they looked was referred to as 'he' and this enabled me to judge how I felt about being seen and referred to as

A New Man

male. The answer was that I felt simply brilliant.

I started to settle into my masculine identity and I had many discussions with fellow trans men at the support group. I made further changes to my appearance. First, I tried to flatten my chest with wide bandages but this was very uncomfortable and they rode up. Then I wore two bras. Then I ordered a very effective flattening sports tight bra online from the US. Later I bought a realistic packer to put in my pants to give the appearance of male genitalia and to give me the feeling of having it. I had tried a small dildo but this was too hard and it was also far too visible as I embarrassingly realised on a night out. These packers were manufactured packages of penis and testicles in one mould, made of soft plastic, known as 'cyberskin'. This, I reassured myself, was only temporary: I was going to have my own full package soon, I hoped. I also bought an STPD (a stand to pee device) as I resented having to wait ages for the cubicle to become free in the men's toilets. It was a great feeling being able to use the urinals. Some products tried to incorporate the peeing devices, into the packer but using these were difficult to master.

I carried my STPD in my underpants to use. I found it relatively easy to use but there was an embarrassing moment when it fell out when I was playing squash. You also had to ensure you didn't drink too much as it was all too easy to end up pissing over your trousers instead.

I don't remember the first time I switched going to men's toilets but it was an easy transition. In fact, I had always had more problems going to women's toilets than men's as sometimes I was told to leave due to my non-feminine appearance.

I wasn't sure how to go about starting the hormones. David advised me to go private to get my diagnosis and hormones as it was easier and less traumatic, and not that expensive and others agreed. It was explained if I went the 'NHS route' that I would be forced to do the dreaded 'real life test'. This is where you're supposed to demand and expect people treat you as male, refer to you with a male name etc. all without having any secondary male characteristics like a deep voice and facial hair, which is practically impossible. Theoretically this was

Becoming a 'New Man'

meant to assist people decide whether changing gender was appropriate for them or not, whereas it was often just sheer humiliation.

Private gender psychiatrists, of which there were two in the UK, used different methods. A common one was to try hormones for a short period and then people who felt comfortable with the psychological and sexual effects were considered more likely to be candidates for hormones full-time and then later full gender surgical reassignment.

I had to admit the so-called real-life test did not appeal in the slightest. Truth be told, I had already taken a very long real-life test: being a woman for years. That did not fit well at all and caused me huge problems, despite the best efforts of my lovers, who thought the only problem was that I had internalised society's hatred of women. I didn't have a problem with other women's bodies, though, only my own.

I read and heard about the physical changes caused by taking hormones. That was all very clear: higher sex drive, deepening tone of the voice, menstruation stopping, increased genitalia size, increased muscle mass, facial hair, higher body temperature etc. But what wasn't explained so much was the psychological changes and how people would treat you differently.

In a book by an American trans man, Loren Cameron, I saw photos of trans men with before and after portraits alongside stories told in their own words. The visual transformations were stunning, any concern that I wouldn't appear male vanished. In this book, I also discovered a trans man called Max Wolf Valerio. Max explained how it took him years to feel comfortable as a heterosexual man from his background in the lesbian feminist community. It was comforting to read that there were others like me from a similar place, and I strongly identified with him.

I next bought a hefty sociological book by H. Devor on Female to Male Transsexuals from the 'Gays the Word' book shop in Marchmont Street, Central London. I devoured the 600 pages. A wide range of transsexual men were interviewed in the book and analysed. Reading it confirmed for me that most trans men were not intentionally turning their backs on feminism by transitioning but that they were just being

A New Man

true to themselves.

The statistics were also fascinating. With three quarters saying that they refused to allow their partners (male or female) to penetrate them vaginally seeing it as an essential aspect of female sexuality. It was gratifying to know so many felt like me.

I decided that Andrea Dworkin's view that men's oppression of women was demonstrated and perpetuated by intercourse was too simplistic. I concluded that how you are in bed need not transmit to everyday life, and I realised that fundamentally it was the alliances with men which radical feminists objected to, not the actual sex. They felt that having relationships with men meant providing men with time and energy that should instead be directed towards women. In reality, sex wasn't really the main problem, it was more that sexual relationships drew men and women together. Sex, anyway, is not just about intercourse of course and the pressure on men to perform and for long periods was ignored by this feminist view point; then there are all the different sexual positions that put women in control of the act.

Feeling far more resolved about these issues, more certain and positive about transitioning and being able to still be pro-feminist, I decided to go ahead and I chose the private route. I arranged to have an appointment with the recommended gender-specialist psychiatrist in Earls Court, Dr Russell Reid.

What should I wear, I pondered? Clearly, I wanted to demonstrate I was serious but I also didn't want to go overboard and wear a suit. I settled on just denim jeans, and a black and grey striped shirt with brogues for footwear. I arrived at the address, a red-orange brick building with the offices signed below, down the metal stairway. I went downstairs and rang the bell with apprehension. Straightaway a woman answered. She appeared to be the receptionist. I wondered if she was trans. She was very busy, sealing envelopes and just asked me to take a seat.

I sat down on the brown leather sofa then looked around and absorbed the atmosphere. It was quite a sombre setting with books on shelves, artworks on the wall decorated in light brown wallpaper. There were some leaflets of various trans groups available. The one slightly strange feature was a statue of a naked person. Was it a man or a woman? I can't remember.

I waited and thought about what I would say, what I'd be asked; time ticked on and on. I noticed after a while that I'd been there for 45 minutes and still hadn't been called and then the receptionist had to leave. She said I'd be called out by Dr Reid and that he was running late. This wasn't good, I was never patient at the best of times and I had made a special effort to be right on time. Finally, after an hour, I was seen. Dr Reid was very apologetic and friendly, and we got down to business. I didn't care anymore about the long wait.

He asked me detailed questions about my past. It was interesting as it was the first time that a professional pointed out that my mum and I were pretty co-dependent until she had re-married for the third time when I was in my late twenties. It was true that I was the first person she turned to for advice and support and I felt a big weight lift off my shoulders when she remarried to a calm, stable and kind man. When the full detailed letter was produced, it was sent to both me and my GP. I showed it to my dad and he was very unhappy that he hadn't been mentioned at all but the truth was that he had hardly featured in my childhood, much as I loved him and wished that he had. Colin, of course, had no idea that I was planning to transition. I hadn't seen him for years as I'd stopped all contact with him after I had moved to the squat in Kennington. A postcard was once forwarded to my flat in Brixton but I never replied. There didn't seem any point. I felt we were evens.

After I went back again for another appointment I had my diagnosis fairly quickly. We covered a lot of ground including my sexual history. It was straightforward, as I was pretty much a textbook female to male transsexual. Dr Reid gave me a slip of paper. On it stated, along with Dr Reid's medical credentials, address and date,

'To whom it may concern, this confirms that Charlie Kiss is having treatment for female to male transsexualism. Wearing men's clothes and taking male hormones is part of this process and is quite appropriate.'

A New Man

Dr Reid advised me to carry this with me at all times, so that when using male toilets etc, I could produce this in event of being challenged by authorities. I did carry it around for ages but I never needed to show it. Still, it was a validating having the bit of paper.

When I walked out of the psychiatrist's gender clinic in Earls Court on 27th September 2002, now 37, with a confirmed diagnosis, I was deliriously happy. Surely if I was that happy then it was obvious that this was the right thing to do, I thought to myself, to end my years and years of being unhappy in the wrong body and persona.

I went for a special celebratory drink with a friend. I felt on the road to a new life. I started to tell those closest to me. My mum to my surprise, worked it out very quickly before I had a chance to tell her. When staying with me she detected a change and she turned to me and said, 'So you want to be a boy now?'

'Yes,' I replied surprised at her perceptiveness, 'I'm pretty sure I do but it isn't an easy process, it could take a very long time and there would be difficult operations.'

'Well, other people have done it and have managed fine, so I don't see why you can't.' Marta replied.

Marta coincidentally had a friend in Bristol, Trevor, transition to male just prior to this, though I hadn't met him since he'd transitioned. I think she found this reassuring seeing him become much happier and at ease with himself. In fact, Marta was extremely enthusiastic about the prospect of me becoming a man. I found that slightly concerning as if she thought it was better to be male than a lesbian, but as my mother she knew me better than anyone and she obviously felt it was the right thing to do.

My dad had a different take on things. He was worried about the hormones and surgery and he thought I should just be a masculine woman. Over a pint in a Kilburn pub, I protested, 'Dad, it isn't that easy, there might be an illusion of acceptance of masculine women and also of unisex culture, but it's actually very hard fitting in society and in any case, that's not the point. The point is that I've never felt particularly female and I've never been able to cope having a female body.'

I didn't want to have to discuss the personal intimate details of my sex life with my dad.

'Yes, I suppose so and it's true that you never looked quite right in a skirt,' was his response.

The truth of the matter was that if it was only a matter of what I looked like and what I wore, I probably could have carried on as 'a masculine woman' but I had a fundamental disconnect with my body and I wanted to appear as I really was, a man, and towards both women and men outwardly too.

My sister was quite pleased about this turn of events and jokingly remarked that all those lesbian bars that I had dragged her to when younger could have been avoided and that we could have gone out together to straight bars instead.

Most of my friends were ultimately accepting. Kristin had no problems at all and was encouraging. Rebekah was concerned about whether I was doing the right thing but then later felt comfortable about it. Jane, questioned me extensively about whether it was necessary to go that far, and some lesbian friends were really shocked that I wanted to have a penis. They couldn't believe it. I didn't want to have to explain or justify it any more but there were still more people who needed to know.

I had to let everyone at work know, at Calverts. I decided the fairest and simplest way to do this was to tell everyone at the same time hence I chose to announce it at the main monthly meeting. I prepared a statement and I read it out explaining that in three months hence, from January 2003, I wished to be referred to using male pronouns only and that I would also soon be taking time off for surgery. After I had finished reading there was silence then one man punched his fist in the air in delight by the news. He saw it as radical. I didn't agree. This wasn't a choice, it was similar to being gay, I tried to explain to him.

At least it wasn't a negative reaction, and overall people at the co-op accepted it although it did take one man, months to stop referring to me as 'she', which I found extremely annoying. I spoke to the woman responsible for the HR side of things. She assumed that I would be

A New Man

taking annual leave for the expected operations, which was a disappointment. She said that the operations were elective. I was shocked and tried to explain why they weren't. I couldn't help pointing out that with so many of the workers still smoking at the time, they were in effect choosing medical treatment more than I was. I had to explain to her that it would be discriminatory not to allow me to have sick time off for the operations.

It would have been better to have had unconditional support but that's the pressure in a co-operative, all the workers own the business and so it follows that anyone needing time off is problematic. Given I would likely have to undertake a lot of operations I felt it might be better to find a new job.

I also thought it would be good to have a brand-new start where no one would know of my former female self. I felt an overwhelming urge to hide so that people would never know what I looked like before transitioning but this was impossible. I began to look for a new job.

The next step was to obtain hormonal treatment; the testosterone is usually administered by injection. Once I had received the official diagnosis and report of gender dysphoria on paper from the private psychiatrist, I went to my GP to request the testosterone treatment as had been indicated as necessary in the report and waited.

I had been told this was a crucial crossroads. If I had troubles with my GP then I could end up being on private treatment for ever. Happily, she accepted it and could see no problem with me receiving the hormonal treatment. Another success. I felt like I was walking on air when I left the GP's surgery. Two weeks later I was given my first testosterone injection by the nurse. Almost immediately I had a warm urgent sexual sensation, which I'd read about but it was still a surprise. More testosterone injections followed every two weeks, and unusually after only my fourth shot, my voice dropped significantly, which was wonderful. Over the next few months, I developed the male characteristics I had desired and envied all my life. I revelled in the gradual changes, such as having a thicker neck and more masculine face shape. I started to have more energy and I had a renewed enthusiasm for life.

178

Some changes weren't particularly welcome. For example, I was in the bath one day and I noticed a loose hair on my shoulder and I tried to remove it before realising that it wasn't loose and in fact long hairs were growing out of my shoulders. I was turning into a werewolf. The two things I wasn't particularly keen on, obtaining hair all over my body and losing hair on top were to be the less welcome aspects of becoming male.

I asked my GP if it would be alright to inject myself as the appointments were very difficult to arrange and organise with having to leave work. Again, she was accommodating and said once the nurse had shown me how to do this, she could see no reason why I couldn't inject myself. I first had to do it myself in front of a nurse. I tried to concentrate on the mechanics of how the body works and what was required, to make it easier for me to inject myself with the massive needle. The nurse, a gay man, was very supportive and encouraging. I felt a wave of solidarity when once I'd arrived late for my injection appointment and he was on his way out, but he saw me, took off his jacket and returned to the treatment room to give me my injection.

Patience is not a strong point of mine, but on the plus side it does spur you on to sort things out. After the hormonal treatment was well underway, I focussed on getting the chest surgery organised. I felt humiliated having breasts even though I had bought the best crunching binder possible and I wore baggy shirts and hunched my shoulders to help hide the unmentionables. I wanted to have the chest surgery as soon as possible. This meant I'd have to go back to Dr Reid, the private psychiatrist to obtain approval.

Four months after my first shot of testosterone, I was excitedly making my way by tube to a private hospital, 'The Wellington' in St John's Wood, Central London, for chest reconstruction surgery. In other words, my breast tissue was to be removed and my nipples removed, resized and reattached. I had taken out a loan as I didn't have savings for the cost of the surgery, which was about £3,300. I was sure it was worth it rather than having to wait years for it to be funded by the NHS. I didn't want to suffer the summer in stifling heat wearing bind-

A New Man

ers and long baggy shirts and I was really fed up with hunching my shoulders.

The operation was an amazing experience. Not many people understand the joy trans people feel on going into hospital to get things sorted. I was in for one night only. The operation was in the late afternoon. Afterwards I phoned friends up completely elated, letting them know I was alright and that it had been a success. I was on the top floor and at night looked out at the beautiful lights across London.

Katie and I got back together, after only four months of being apart. We felt it was worth giving it another go and for me I had the added incentive of an increased sex drive as well as still feeling a lot for her. I was going through a second puberty and had become obsessed with sex and could think of little else. I was spending a lot of time on dating and erotic websites. I posted erotic stories and I sent messages to the women on these sites and also tried to meet someone through dating sites but had not managed to.

Katie also felt that the relationship should be more about the person and our personalities rather than what our bodies were like. It was an admirable sentiment. I had my doubts as to whether she could change and like my new masculine body. I had never been attracted to masculine bodies myself. I, of course, didn't have to change how I felt about her physically but we decided to give it another go, embarking on a very different journey and relationship together.

Katie then had to contend with my pre-occupation with the changes that were taking place within me physically and emotionally and towards me socially. My muscles increased in size, I became stronger, I had more energy, my body temperature changed, I was warmer, I discovered I sweated a hell of lot more, and I wanted the duvet off whereas Katie wanted it on. My back itched like mad. My smooth skin disappeared, and in its place, I became hairy pretty much all over and pimply on my thighs.

The degree of increase in muscular strength was a surprise. A couple of years later at an LGBT afternoon fete next to the Vauxhall tavern, I was part of a tug of war team made up exclusively of trans men, and we

Becoming a 'New Man'

did really well, far exceeding the expectations of ourselves and onlookers.

I felt more at ease when we went to pubs. For the first time in my life, I experienced heterosexual privilege. People didn't give us a second glance. After so many years of being worn down by inquisitive or hostile looks it was a welcome change.

Katie came and collected me from the private hospital the morning after my chest surgery. Thinking I was being ripped off, I refused the offer of powerful painkillers that I'd been prescribed. The pills seemed far too expensive to me and I thought I'd be just fine and manage without them. A few hours later I was in extreme pain. I also discovered there is an amazing number of tasks, you use your chest muscles for, including even turning a tap. It was agony sitting up from lying down so for about a week I slept sitting up propped up by pillows.

Katie stayed with me for a few days and looked after me which and then Marta took over for a few days. I felt loved, having their support. Dad and his new partner came over for tea one afternoon too. I was off work for a total of three weeks to recover.

It was wonderful having a new masculine looking chest. I had scars but I didn't mind. It's practically impossible to have no scars at all for chest surgery unless you are ultra-small and can have liposuction. I discovered that unlike a lot of people, my scars were quite prominent and didn't heal well. Other people's scars disappeared almost completely, mine didn't and my chest hair didn't hide the scars either.

Another obvious sign of being trans was that I had been proud of having the small size 38A when I appeared female, as it showed I had a large back and smallish breasts. I had also complained that my erectile tissue between my legs was so small. No one else I knew said similar things.

I liked the contours of my new chest, my shirts fitted so much better. My nipples had been made much smaller both in area and height and they reacted naturally to cold and touch. People sometimes asked if the sensation was the same as before but I had no idea, I had nothing to compare as I didn't touch them myself nor allow anyone else to.

A New Man

Before I started on hormones I knew it was important for me to go the whole way to change my body completely to a male one as far as possible. I, like many trans people, have pondered over the possibility of genital transplants, but the thing is I felt it would be better to have a penis constructed out of my own skin and tissue. In fact, I had read that often transplants are not successful psychologically, and I can imagine having such an intimate area transplanted would be significantly more difficult, never mind the prospect of having to take immunosuppressant drugs forever.

Once I had established for definite, though, that it was possible to remove the vagina and womb and have a penis, testicles and have an ability to have erections, I was going to do everything I could to make it happen. This surgery was going to be a much bigger process. I made an appointment for a consultation with the UK phalloplasty team and waited. Months later at the consultation, they said they should be able to get my NHS funding sorted out. They showed me very impressive-looking results on their laptop. I would be having the forearm method - where they take skin from your arm to create a penis and use skin from your inner arm to create a urethra. As the months, then years passed, I became frustrated and did more research.

Although it was possible to get the lower surgery in the UK paid for by the NHS, I had heard of people having to have multiple operations coming in and out of hospital every six months needing revision operations. The minimum was five operations if everything went to plan and that excluded the hysterectomy. I had also seen a variety of results, some very good, some really poor.

Having many operations didn't appeal and would also be very difficult with work to organise all the time off needed. I already had had to remind my fellow directors at the worker's co-op of my legal right to have time off for this surgery. But I felt responsible about the co-op. I had returned to work only three weeks after my chest operation, but in retrospect, I really needed four weeks. I had difficulty loading the production scheduling board as I couldn't raise my arms.

So, I carried out intensive research on the internet on lower surgery

Becoming a 'New Man'

for trans men and discovered that in Europe it was possible to have all the main operations done in two operations only reducing the time needed off for the surgery. The best teams seemed to be in Belgium, Holland and Germany but in Holland you had to be a resident for the surgery and in Belgium, the waiting list was over two years.

I looked on the German website and dreamed of the possibilities. They did practically everything in one go, the hysterectomy, removal of the vagina, creation of a penis and testicles, the whole works. There would only be one more operation, which would be for the erectile prostheses and testicular silicone implants.

It was everything I could hope for and was everything I had dreamed of. It seemed perfect but I would need about 45,000 Euros. I had no idea as to how I was going to get that sort of money. I stayed up at night trying to work out how I would get the money to cover the cost. In Germany, I also read, they only required you to be on hormones for six months prior to the operation rather than the two years I heard was necessary for Belgium, where you could also get all the main operations in one go.

So meanwhile I had to cope. Once in the Black Cap, a gay bar in Camden Town, I was using a urinal when a bloke looked over and he looked at me startled after he had seen my plastic STP (stand to pee) device. I didn't say anything, but I left the toilet wishing that the FTM London group didn't always go to a gay bar for drinks post-meeting although there were advantages especially considering some of us looked masculine but didn't quite pass. The Black Cap was welcoming to everyone.

It took five years after my first testosterone shot before I had the lower surgery. I waited and waited for the private UK phalloplasty team in London to sort out the NHS issue. The UK team had set up a private organisation and then charged the NHS for the work. They said I shouldn't need to see an NHS psychiatrist, but after two years of barely no contact and delays, I gave up on them and I decided to leave their list and take a chance on getting the funding approval via the official route, which meant going right back to square one.

A New Man

I joined the long list for the NHS gender clinic to get the formal NHS diagnosis in order to try to get NHS funding, first having to see a local gender psychiatrist, then two more at the gender clinic at the Charing Cross hospital. This took about a year and a half. I reasoned I could try and see if the NHS would pay for treatment in the Belgian hospital; it was in Europe after all and if not, I had not lost anything, though the more I read about the Belgian team, the more determined I was.

I had heard that one person had managed to have the surgery in Belgium on the basis of long waiting lists but there was scant information about this. I figured I didn't have much to lose. But finding anything out was a long, drawn-out process. It made me angry reading tabloid newspapers implying that it's easy to get a 'sex change on the NHS'.

One advantage to having a long wait prior to the surgery was that I was able to have extensive laser treatment to remove the dark hair from my arm. Obviously, it would be an advantage not to have a hairy penis. But there was also a more serious side, removing hair and hair follicles meant that a blockage caused by salts in the urine passing through would be far less likely. Blockages were serious and usually meant revision surgery. Happily, my laser treatment turned out to be successful.

21

Living as a Man

It takes about two years to fully transition, to go from looking androgynous to undoubtedly male. After this time had passed, I lost any outward appearance of being female and I had to learn fast how to behave and to understand why people related to me differently. I felt wary and unsure. If I put a foot wrong, then I'd soon get told off. I didn't get any encouragement when I did things as I should because it was expected.

The intervening period before completely passing as male was awkward too. Encountering people who didn't know if I was male or female was especially trying. A salesman in a department store said, 'Can I help you, sir? I mean madam, I mean sir, sorry...'

To get through this stage, a lot of trans people try and be more obviously male (or female if trans women) and use more gender specific clothes or other indicators to try and to help people out. With local shops, it was harder knowing what to do as it didn't seem appropriate to explain to absolutely everyone what was happening to me. Fortunately for me the local shop I used the most, went through a change of management and so had new people serving. The man at the Dry Cleaners asked me if I had sister which was simultaneously awkward and amusing.

I paid a visit to a man who had transitioned a few years before me. I was curious because I had heard he also had had the 'Brenda' treatment when he'd been young at Greenham too. He, however, hadn't been affected as I was and brushed it off when I asked him about his experiences. I wondered if that was because he was comfortable with an S&M identity. Anyway, we had a good talk about transitioning and surgery and then when we said goodbye, he held out his hand and we shook hands. I'd never done that before – shake hands with a friend to say goodbye. It occurred to me that from now on, this was going to be

A New Man

standard, shaking hands instead of hugging.

It felt like a special moment and I saw, with other trans men, our behaviour quickly assumed men's standard behaviour. When going out drinking we all stood around for ages holding our pints instead of sitting down. I wasn't someone who cared necessarily for following convention, but some of it was welcome, such as not having to hug people all the time, as I found enforced intimacy could be overwhelming.

Unlike boys going through their puberty, Trans men only have the two years to adjust and understandably mistakes are made. The other problem for me was that I looked like a very young man, almost as young as a teenage boy and it wasn't easy moving from being treated with the respect granted to a thirty-seven-year-old woman to being treated like a teenage boy.

I had mistakenly thought it would still be okay to go on holiday with my mum, after only a year on hormones, this was a music tour through the south of the USA that had been planned for a while. I had assumed correctly that I would have transitioned enough to appear male but what I had not taken on board was that I would look under twenty. Everywhere I went I had to prove my age, as in many states alcohol can't be served to anyone under twenty-one. I also had to put up with people on the coach party telling me that I shouldn't be listening to their adult conversations and the like. As a teenage boy, my views weren't respected and I was humoured or put down.

On one occasion, I was grabbed and pulled to one side by a woman to make way for another woman entering the lift. I was expected to move out the way most of the time for women. From my former viewpoint, I hadn't noticed this. I had only seen that men occupied space in a territorial manner and that women were afforded less space, now as 'a young man' as it were, I could see that we were expected to move out the way for women and that we were supposed to think of them first.

When travelling on the tube, I saw that if it was crowded, men usually didn't dash to the first available seat, and usually waited to check that a woman didn't want to sit down. This is superficial to the real power and influence men hold in the world, of course, but it was still

Living as a Man

a surprise.

Marta said she wasn't worried any more about me cycling in London. I joked with her about that, as if she didn't care anymore. It was ironic though because if anything, although I'd cycled for years and was experienced, on testosterone I found myself taking more risks. She also took to covering herself up more, previously she'd take her top off in my flat when changing, no problem. I found this funny and I said to her, 'It's me, I'm the same person!'

The challenge after being on testosterone for two years and appearing male was that people expected me to know how to behave. I'm quite sensitive, so I had to come to terms quickly with the fact that people care less about your feelings as a man.

You're expected to take it on the chin. People will say what they think about your appearance and behaviour with no sugar-coating. Now in some respects this was a relief. It used to annoy me intensely when a man would ask If I'd be alright walking down a street on my own with poor lighting but now I also had to accept that there would be fewer allowances in many different instances. The upside was that I would be treated with greater respect, especially by other men, but I had to develop a tougher skin and learn different ways of behaving.

A car drove far too close to me almost driving over my feet as I was walking across the road. In my shock, I reacted instinctively and shouted out, 'Wanker!' to the driver. Had I done this in my past, I would probably have received at the most some equally offensive verbal back, but now things were different. The car screeched to a halt and the driver, a big bloke, got out of the car and started to come after me. He looked like he was about to do me in, he was furious. I turned and ran as fast as I could and mercifully he couldn't be bother to pursue me. I was going to have change fast to avoid getting in some hairy situations.

I saw a black woman being kicked by two white women in a street brawl outside a nightclub in Brighton. I stepped in to try and help the woman being kicked on the ground but suddenly out of nowhere I was pushed and thrown back a couple of metres in the air against a wall by a bloke who obviously didn't want me to intervene, I was temporarily

A New Man

winded. The woman on the ground managed to get up. I went over and asked her if she was okay but she was not impressed by my feeble attempt to help.

So, I learnt quickly as a man you must expect a reaction - and a violent one – in these types of situations from other men and learn how to avoid it. I wondered how often men I knew had got into fights or were beaten up and I asked one of the men at work, he replied 'only once.' I suspected he was an avoider, which I needed to become. Another bloke I met at college had been mugged and attacked many times, largely due to his Pakistani background. Defence I could understand, but this macho lark of violence and the risk of getting your head kicked in wasn't for me. It seemed stupid and reminded me of the time I was supposed to fight with Frankie. I could relate to frustration but sometimes violence by men was about show and power.

My mum and other people changed their behaviour towards me. On one occasion, I had arrived at a restaurant with Marta and I was desperate for the toilet. As soon as we were given a table, I left the table saying, 'Right, I must go to the toilet, I'll be back in a tick.'

On my return, Marta remonstrated with me, 'You should wait and ask if I need to go first before rushing off.' She said. 'You're not being at all polite as a man.'

She also demanded that I stepped in front of her and opened all doors for her, holding them open whilst she walked through. Now I know that a lot of this is old-fashioned and superficial but there is still pressure to do a lot of this sort of thing and it looks rude if you don't. 'Ladies first' is the continual refrain, I hated all that before but it's easier to protest about it if you're a woman, as a man you're considered selfish and rude if you object.

Some of this behaviour is just polite behaviour that everyone should do. But often women don't thank you, instead they expect you to move out of the way or hold the door open for them and then at other times, they look at you as if you're stupid for opening the door for them, patronising in fact, which is what I used to feel. It's hard to know what to do for the best, and I think it's best to err on the over-polite and old-fashioned.

Lots of people wanted me to adopt their ideas of masculinity. Women who described themselves as feminist said to me that if I wanted to pass, I should swear more, which really surprised me. Some of the printers at work encouraged to me to start boxing which I didn't agree with, never mind have any desire to take up.

I was astonished by this and just tried to steer my own course. I felt confident that I wouldn't have any difficulties in presenting as male and that I just had to wait for the testosterone to do its work and didn't worry too much after a while about my mannerisms and way of behaving and so I didn't start swearing more as suggested.

All the new behaviours that would minimise offence or embarrassment had to be learnt very quickly. Before, I could go into a pub and look around properly. As a man, I realised it's a different ball game. If I looked at a man intently then I'd be considered either threatening or gay and if I looked at a woman, this was perceived as me being sexually interested in them. For the first few months I had my head down.

To my dismay, I could also rarely look at children for longer than a few seconds without the mother giving me filthy looks and sometimes even moving the child away. If I saw a lesbian or gay couple, I felt an urge to smile or reassure them that that all was fine by me, but this didn't work well either, I just appeared like a pervert then. It seemed instead that the most appropriate and less problematic way to behave was to be like your average heterosexual man and I found myself adopting this early on.

When I told my dad about my transitioning, he said I couldn't have chosen a worse time, and that masculinity was not currently fashionable. He was right in one sense but I feel that masculinity is changing for the better and for the benefit of everyone. It's good for example that now men are learning to cook and fathers look after children more and that more men are aware of the toxic effects of sexism.

I used to look at men suspiciously myself so you could say that I should've expected negative attitudes towards men but I thought it was predominately lesbians who held these views. I hadn't expected almost

A New Man

everyone else to hold men in low regard. It was unpleasant to be suddenly treated in such a negative way and constantly with suspicion but I had to start getting used to it.

I said to Kristin, half-jokingly, 'Shouldn't you welcome me into the wonderful world of heterosexuality?'

'It's not actually that wonderful, I'm afraid,' she replied.

I was beginning to realise this.

Going out for drinks in the West End was an eye-opener. Another male friend and I arrived at a bar, which was completely full except for two seats at a table for four, which was occupied by two women who were chatting to each other.

I asked if we could sit down at the table but the answer was an emphatic 'no'. It was clear they thought we were planning on chatting them up when we just wanted to sit down and talk to each other.

Another time a male friend and I wanted to go into a bar in Leicester Square but the bouncer said that only women or couples could go in. It was so ironic to me. I had been under the false impression that the world would be wider to me as a heterosexual man but it wasn't that straightforward. Also, to go to a lot of clubs I would have to pay whereas women would go in free. Having spent most of my time in the lesbian world, I didn't know any of this. I also discovered in most bars and clubs all the women would stick together and the men would do the same. How were people supposed to meet and get together? I wondered.

Before, as a woman, I would resent men always offering to buy drinks and would offer to buy them drinks instead. I remember vividly after work once, the sales manager offered to buy me and the other women we were with, drinks and food - he brought out his credit card and actually said, 'I've got the power!'

I resented men's power then, but at least as a woman I could challenge it. Now I can't challenge the dynamic. That would be considered rude, but what I've observed to help balance things out is that often there's a bit of a charade that goes on: men often buy the first drinks in a 'showy way', and then women (if they're offering) will buy a second

Living as a Man

drink or, if already in couples, women will sometimes give money to their partners to go to the bar.

But on dates, it's often a different matter. A friend, a trans man, went out on a date with a woman. He bought all the food and drinks in a classy restaurant then right at the end he asked if she would be up for buying him one drink. This didn't go down well at all and other trans men told him he shouldn't have asked her. I agree that on a date things are different but I did feel a bit sorry for him as he'd spent a fortune.

I was finding out just how different the world was for men. It was an altogether different experience just walking through Soho to what it was like when I was perceived as a woman. I had men come up to me and ask what type of sex I was looking for, simply because I was alone and male in Soho. I suspect they wanted only to relive men of money however, as I'd heard from someone who'd been homeless and hung around that area, that there's a scam whereby money is taken off tourists and they're given keys to non-existent flats having been given addresses of where to go.

I saw a documentary about an older woman who had transitioned from male in her late 60s. She said she was now really happy and remarked, 'women are so friendly and I have loads of friends now.' Well the opposite is true for trans men. Men don't share much with each other or support each other. Trans men probably do a bit more with each other at first but as we get more integrated into society, most of us start behaving in the same way as other men.

Emotionally, I changed. For most of my adult female life I cried and cried often. I think the power of hormones is underestimated, for I basically stopped crying. Was it just the hormones working? It seemed so. It certainly wasn't that I suddenly thought I had to act like a man. Before hormones, which stopped the periods immediately, the night before a period started it was almost guaranteed that I'd cry. Crying at least two to three times a week dropped dramatically to only about twice a year.

My moods were much less volatile. This had upsides in that it was good for me to be more levelled emotionally having suffered bi-polar

A New Man

mania disorder, but it also meant I got less excited and overall had less emotional experiences of sadness and euphoria. I didn't – as so many people expected – become more aggressive; in fact, I became much calmer and my anger and aggression all but disappeared.

I tried a feminist men's group. At first, they were reluctant to allow me to join as I didn't hide that fact of being a trans man, but after some consideration, they decided to allow me in. I was disappointed to discover that it was more of mutual therapy group where the men talked about their week. Also crying was greatly encouraged, which I found really odd. They believed crying was repressed, and that it was social conditioning. I begged to differ and they were bemused and not pleased at my assertion that it was mostly hormonal. It was a small group and after two meetings, I had had enough. I'd had years of therapy by this point and didn't feel the need to go to a men's therapy group too.

I began dating. The relationship with Katie had drawn to a close two years after we had got back together. Katie finished the relationship; it was no longer functioning and I didn't object. For one date, which was with a deputy head teacher, I did a similar thing as my friend, I chose what I considered was a good restaurant and quickly paid for everything when she'd gone to the toilet. When she returned, she said that I shouldn't have paid and said,

'Come on, equality and all that!'

I felt a bit silly especially as I'd known she would be earning twice as much as me but I had decided I wanted to pay.

It is expected that men choose where you're meeting for dates. This might seem a given in the heterosexual world and probably not even noticed, but for me it was a big change. Usually they'd expect me to tell them where we'd meet but I would try and give more than one option, so that I wasn't dictating but then they'd reply saying, 'No, you choose.' From straight female friends, I discovered that women get colossal amounts of messages from men on dating sites, it's expected that men make the first move.

In the big scheme of things, the politics of dating are quite trivial of course compared to the real battles that matter in relationships. Men still don't pull their weight in terms of cleaning and housework. The sharing of cooking has improved but we still have a long way to go and then of course there's the income difference and the domestic violence issue.

I think most trans people acknowledge that gender roles can be tiresome and restrictive to people's lives. Personally, I think people should be encouraged to try and learn new things even if they don't conform to the expectation of their gender as different skills can come in handy and makes life more interesting. I also began to learn to cook, late in life but better than never. I know a trans woman who regularly carries out car maintenance and fixes plumbing and the like for others, not worrying if this doesn't help her 'passing' ability. She now experiences what I used to experience – patronising behaviour from staff in bicycle shops. I used to be so insulted when it was presumed by male cycle shop staff that I didn't know what I wanted or what I was talking about. That doesn't happen anymore, I am now given respect in bike shops. I'm now given respect in many situations, the main advantage to being a man. Naturally many trans women, most I would suggest, become feminist if they weren't before as it's obvious when you transition just how differently men and women are treated and many are affronted.

At college, studying economics, I had my first experiences of being around people who knew nothing of my female past. It was satisfying. Although I looked totally male, I still looked very young – about 25 years old rather than 40. Sometimes I was asked personal questions like, 'Do you have a girlfriend?' Once a woman asked me about domestic chores, and I revealed I did my own cooking, ironing etc. She said: 'So you're a new man!' The two meanings of the expression made me smile.

One of the major conundrums I found after transitioning was that I wasn't sure whether I should come out to people I'd meet in various situations who I knew from the past. A lot depends on the situation of course, and how long you're likely to be in their company in this new situation and what your previous relationship was, but I found it, and still do, a difficult ethical dilemma. I felt uncomfortable when I saw

A New Man

someone from the past because I knew a lot about them but they didn't have the faintest idea who I was as obviously my appearance was vastly different.

It felt deceptive. But on the other hand, it just isn't always appropriate to announce your transition in every situation, not everyone takes it very well and ultimately transitioning is acutely personal and coming out as trans to someone you knew before, needs be handled with care, so I try to judge when and where.

A welcome aspect of transitioning was that I began to feel some camaraderie towards men. I remembered how much I liked boys as friends when I was young and it was nice to get it back to some degree and enjoy being around other men though as men there is a big emotional distance. There is a special bond between trans men of course and to some extent with trans women too, from our shared experience of transitioning but it was a real joy to move out from the lesbian separatist world, and to be able to enjoy men's company again.

Surprisingly my attitude towards men's bodies changed drastically too. I could now appreciate men's bodies. I was liberated from my jealousy of their bodies as I had no reason now to be jealous of course.

It also meant I became closer to my dad and I was pleased he had seen me transition. He remarked one day that he was impressed at the transformation. He had been very worried I would change my mind and regret transitioning but I reassured him that was definitely not going to happen.

However, he didn't see me go bald like he had because he died of a sudden heart attack only two years after I started my transition. I wasn't working at the time so I was the first to be told. The telephone rang and I was woken up at 4am. It was very strange because I heard someone say, 'your dad's dead!' I thought it was a very nasty hoax call by some cruel person. In my half-asleep state, I responded angrily saying, 'no he isn't!' But the voice at the end of the phone persisted and said it again and then it slowly and horribly dawned on me that the voice was one I recognised, that of Daphne, Dad's partner and I went completely cold.

Living as a Man

Daphne explained Dad had had a heart attack and that the police and ambulance staff were there. I just could not believe it. She asked me tearfully if I would be coming down. I replied, 'I'm on my way.'

I was in a daze long afterwards. He was never ill, so he never went to the doctors and was completely unaware he was at risk. He was slim, cycled a lot, was very active and of course he had been vegetarian since he was 23 so on the face of things he seemed ultra healthy.

I wrote a piece and read it out at the funeral. I said he wasn't late this time, he was early – early to his death. It's strange but I felt released in a way, released from being disappointed. I'd always wanted to be closer to him, to have spent more time with him, just the two of us but it was rarely possible. Later I found a letter from my mum to Dad when I was about 20, saying I was very like him and that I would really like to spend some time with him, but he had other younger children that took precedent. We had missed our chance of a good father-son relationship, despite being so similar. The closest I got to him was when we both discussed depression and suicide. I understood and empathised with him with kindness when he had been ill and he acknowledged that.

His death put things into perspective and reminded me that it is more important to be true to yourself than anything else in life.

22

Surgery in Belgium

I had had consultations in Belgium two years earlier, which included seeing yet another psychiatrist. I passed the report from the private psychiatrist to the friendly Belgian Gender Psychiatrist, which she accepted; however, she was very concerned that I had suffered mania. My heart sank at this because for a moment I thought she wouldn't approve the operation. I explained as calmly as I could that the mental illness was over twelve years previously, and that I had been stable all that time. She then recounted a tale of a patient who had some mental difficulties who had ripped their new penis off. That was quite a horrifying tale and I assured her that I would not be doing anything like that and I would be fine.

On 4th May 2007, I received confirmation from the NHS funding commissioner that I would receive funding for the operation in Belgium. I was ecstatic. It was the best feeling I think I've ever experienced. The operation was expected to cost about half of the cost the UK team charged the NHS. Whilst I am sure this was a factor in granting the funding, it was a significant breakthrough as I was the first trans man in the UK to have obtained the funding to go to Belgium because of the new 'patient choice' pathway rather than due to long waiting lists.

It did take quite a few letters and my GP also helped. I had to explain why I believed the surgery was more suitable for my needs. I provided documentation from Belgium on the cost and the techniques. The Belgian team had also agreed unusually to carry out a hysterectomy for me during the same operation as I hadn't had it done yet which would mean less scarring too.

My mum and I had been trying to work out how we could pay for the operation if we were not granted NHS funding through loans and savings, but it was a colossal amount and such a massive relief not to

Surgery in Belgium

have to try and obtain it. The operation is known as a radial forearm phalloplasty. In other words, crudely put, making a penis from your forearm skin. The first phalloplasty (although skin from the abdomen was used in this case) had been developed by the British surgeon Harold Gilles during the second world war for soldiers who had lost their genitals in battle. The first trans man in the world to undergo this surgery from Harold Gilles was Michael Dillon who had the first operation of thirteen in 1945. Now this had been reduced to only two operations, at least in Europe. The first to create the penis and scrotum, the second to insert an erectile implant and silicon testicular implants. I would be under general anaesthetic for about eight hours whilst two teams of surgeons would be working simultaneously, one working on my arm, creating a urethra (pee tube) from the most hair free part of my inner arm and then penis from the outer part of my arm.

The other team would be working at the recipient area for the penis, after the womb, vagina, et al. would be removed. The surgeons would connect all the tiny nerves in my new penis to the base as well as connect to the thigh nerve so that I would feel pain if say, I caught it in a zip and crucially they would also connect the pudendal nerve which is present in both men and women, at the base of the penis in order that I would be able to achieve orgasms.

A lot of people ask about the orgasms. I have been asked, 'Are they as good as they were before?' To my mind this demonstrates a lack of understanding of being trans. I had huge difficulties using the body I had to have orgasms, especially with other people. It's almost impossible to compare. The important aspect to note is that, yes, it's possible and yes, it's enjoyable.

I had left Calverts and the printing industry after six years, to start afresh in a new working environment. My employer was now a local government authority and it had good sick leave policies, which meant that the pressure was taken off me and I could be discreet. This, in addition to transitioning, was a bonus from having moved away from the printing industry as I wanted to be able to recover without the fear of losing my job and not to suffer financially.

A New Man

In the month leading up to the operation, I had two chest x-rays, and an ECG to test my heart in England to confirm that I was in a fit state to undergo such a major eight-hour long operation. The surgery date was set for the Monday 24th September 2007. Marta came over with me on the Eurostar on the Saturday. We had a slap-up meal in the posh part of Gent that night. I had a pint of beer, which would be my last for a very long time, and then I had to go without food for 30 hours to clear my whole system out.

That Sunday afternoon I entered the hospital and after being allocated a bed, I said goodbye to my mum by the exit to the lifts on the fifth floor, where the plastic surgery recovery ward was. There was no one else about, it was eerily quiet and I was nervous for the first time but it was too late to change my mind. I thought of all the people I had known who had had many operations and complications and I was dreading the possibility of a future of continual operations but there wasn't any going back. What had I let myself in for?

At 6am, after practically no sleep, the door opened and the bed I was in was wheeled to the operating theatre. All the medical team were there with their masks on. They put a cover over my mouth and nose, I was told to breathe in and I was given anaesthesia by gas.

The next day, sometime in the afternoon, I was wheeled into the recovery unit. It was unbearable. There was so much noise: beeping of machines, crashing of beds, nurses talking, shouting. It felt like hell. I was exhausted and so desperate for peace and quiet. I couldn't move, my throat was sore, my face was hot. I threw up. Nurses came over, I desperately wanted something to drink as I was unbelievably thirsty but I wasn't allowed to drink water. A nurse gave me a spray bottle of water so that I could spray my hot face and horrendous dry throat with a cool spray of liquid. I held onto that bottle gratefully and the nurse transformed into an angel. I was later given a wash and had to pull myself gradually to one side with one arm which wasn't easy at all and I was pushed from the other side.

Later I was shown my new equipment below, I didn't know what to say. It all looked okay. A temperature strip had been affixed to my new penis, but I was in hell and couldn't really take anything in. Everything seemed surreal.

It wasn't for another eight hours or so until I was returned to my room. The rooms had two beds. I was sharing with an older man who was in the intensive ward for two leg amputations. My mum came and visited me as soon as she was allowed after the operation. She said I looked totally washed out. She had been in the hospital chapel praying for hours whilst I had been operated on. I then had to have gas extracted from my stomach as I got severe abdominal pains. I was told I had some left over in my stomach from the operation. A tube was stuck up my nose and then down into my stomach which was a strange feeling but I was relieved when the pain had stopped.

My roommate only spoke Flemish, so my smattering of French and German was of no use and we couldn't communicate. With the curtain between us most of the time I didn't see his face either. Everyone on the wing was in intensive care so no one was physically able to get up from their bed and I was told I would have to lie flat on my back on the bed for eight solid days. For the first few days the lower half of my body was under a cage to keep the blankets off my new appendage, and to keep the area dry and at the right temperature. The next few days, I was in a lot of pain. The worst pain was in the new scrotum area, and no wonder, the whole area had been masterfully reconfigured.

The food in the hospital was mundane with far too much bread and yoghurt. Being vegetarian, (I had decided to become vegetarian and risk the wrath of my mum 12 years earlier) meant that there wasn't much variety for me in Belgium and I thought of how much more careful we are in the UK to accommodate the many different religions and different dietary needs.

Not being able to move, I felt like a prisoner forced to lie on my back for days on end. I was completely dependent on the nurses for every need and bodily function. It was tiresome having to stay in bed for hours and hours. I'd brought a few books over to read but most were too heavy to rest on my front. I did, however thoroughly enjoy reading the recently-released 'The Story of CRASS,' which I'd saved for

A New Man

the occasion.

On the seventh day, I was given permission to get up and to walk but, not having put any weight on my feet for so long, my legs were weak and wobbly. Eventually I managed a few steps and soon I could walk to the end of the corridor - extremely slowly - just about coping with the piercing pain between my legs.

The next step was to wean myself off the catheter and learn to urinate through my new penis. This was a gradual process and I had to keep a chart of how much urine I produced through the catheter and compare that with how much came through my new penis, the idea that eventually there would be zero coming through the catheter. This transfer from the catheter wasn't going fast enough for my liking but then one afternoon, without any warning, I suddenly produced a huge arc of urine in the cubicle which was a shock and a delight and it wasn't long afterwards that the catheter was removed.

I kept in contact with friends by texting them all at the same time, which kept me occupied and made me feel less alone but I consequently ran up a mobile phone bill of over £400. I didn't have many visitors during my stay in hospital. Justina came by train from Amsterdam for a weekend and Joe, a trans friend from England, also came over.

After having a physiotherapist show me exercises to do for my donor arm (the arm which had been weakened from having the tissue removed), I was ready to leave the hospital. Everything had gone smoothly. I left hospital on the day I expected to, exactly two and a half weeks after the operation. I had also met some other trans men who were from France, Belgium and America and had some laughs with them before I left. The Belgium team are highly sought after by trans men the world over, for their high-quality lower surgery.

Marta came and collected me from the hospital by taxi and we went to an apartment which I'd booked in advance. It was just one large room with a toilet and kitchen built into it. Here Marta made me egg and chips and baked beans with ice cream for pudding and this meal was exquisite.

I could just about walk but slower than a tortoise as it was extremely painful. I had a horrible fear, that the operation had been unsuccessful and that I would forever be in acute pain down below. I rested for ten days in the apartment, whilst a district nurse came to the flat every day to renew the ointment and dressings on my arm and my leg. My donor arm was in a pretty bad state, very raw and I was convinced I had an infection with all the strange colours but the nurse reassured me that it was fine for this stage of recovery. Having a severe scar on your arm is undoubtedly the drawback of having a forearm phalloplasty. I was going to have to stop wearing T shirts if I wanted to avoid questions and comments about my arm. After the last outpatient appointment, I was given the all clear to go home and we returned to London via Eurostar. I had been out of the country for a whole month.

Overall I was satisfied with how it had all turned out and very grateful for the people within the NHS and the specialist Belgian team who enabled it to happen.

I had one scare a couple of weeks afterwards. I had contracted cellulitis, which is a very serious infection which could result in actual skin and tissue disappearing. It was above where my new penis had been attached. I had taken a photo of the red area and posted it to a trans men's internet group for advice and instantly had health professions from the site telling me to go to A&E urgently. I heeded their advice and made sure I went to the A&E of the hospital where I knew trans men were operated on so that I wouldn't be such an unusual specimen, which turned out to be a good move. I was in hospital for two nights whilst I was given intravenous anti-biotics which worked and the infection was eradicated.

A year later, I went back to Belgium for the erectile hydraulic device and for the testicular silicone implants. I had some reservation as to whether I should go ahead with the erectile device as there were many complications reported with this aspect of the surgery. The alternatives however were not very satisfactory, one possible solution I had read would be to wrap a bandage around your penis, then put on a condom and this was supposed to make it hard enough to penetrate. It wasn't. Another gimmick which also didn't work was a plastic wrap-around

A New Man

device. So, I decided to go ahead with the operation for the hydraulic implant and the testicle fillers.

It's talked about less but having testicle silicone implants and a full scrotum is a great feeling, sensually and psychologically. The Belgian urologist Professor Hoebeke perfected a technique of being able to create a forward separate scrotum which is now copied by other phalloplasty surgeons. After these operations, though I had decided this had to be the end of it all. There are always extras that can be sought to resolve slight imperfections but I had had enough operations.

What I found fascinating about trans men's surgery was that non-trans people had very high expectations, people around me who seemed to be relatively intelligent and knew the basics of biology would ask me if I could have erections naturally and one even asked if I could ejaculate. Of course, ejaculation isn't possible.

Trans men's penises can be large but crucially they don't enlarge when erect. It took some time getting used to my new equipment and knowing how and where to place it in my pants. The surgeons said it was important to change position a lot in the first month or two following surgery. A friend told me never to put it down a trouser leg because in his words, I'd 'frighten old ladies'. Following surgery, the area is usually swollen so you have to re-adjust too when you realise it's not quite as big you thought it would be. I wasn't bothered as I have never wanted a huge one, I just felt more complete that I ever had. What was female about my body now? Okay maybe my chromosomes were XX, but that was about it.

Feeling much more assured of myself physically, I returned to the world of online dating. This was still problematic and stressful knowing that I would have to reveal that I was trans to prospective partners. I wasn't sure whether to state it on my profile though most people advised me not to. A friend who had transitioned in the 80s said I should wait until I know that there is mutual interest, and I could see his point. Why should I reveal something very personal about myself, making myself vulnerable before knowing anything especially personal about them? Also, many people would dismiss you out of hand

Surgery in Belgium

before just seeing you as a person. But I found it really hard not being open. I tried to wait, but when I felt there was mutual interest and I liked them, then sometimes I revealed all on the first date.

This usually proved to be a mistake. On one occasion, the woman's jaw was dropped in shock, then she announced that she had thought I was normal (she incidentally had told me she was bisexual) proceeded to examine my hands and then declared that they were small and therefore a bit of a giveaway. Other times, women just blocked me as soon as they'd got home, which hurt.

I knew a couple of trans men who'd had sex without telling their partners beforehand but I didn't think I could do that. And now with a couple of recent court cases deciding 'deception about gender' was an imprisonable offence, I felt it was a good thing that I hadn't proceeded down that road. (At the time of writing, however, there have been no instances, as far as I'm aware, of post-transition trans men being convicted) Later I switched to being completely open and writing it on my profile thus limiting the possibility of unpleasant reactions and rejections based on being trans.

I met someone and I was dreading having to tell her of my 'condition' but as I could see things were developing, I knew I couldn't leave it too late either so I told her on our third date. I simply said I needed to tell her something that could drastically alter how she would see me. It wasn't very easy but I had to just come out with it and I said I was transsexual, female to male. She hardly blinked which was hugely refreshing and more to the point, she was still interested.

My new girlfriend was heterosexual, independent and strong minded, we were quite competitive with one another but there was little stifling gender stereotyping, thankfully. I am sure I would feel weird fulfilling a stereotypical role doing DIY, taking the rubbish out, whilst she was inside cooking. It was wonderful not to have to declare any parts of my body off limits as I did in the past and an absolute joy to have her hands touch me all over my chest, a part of my body that had never received any affection. Nowhere was out of bounds. I was free at last to be myself, as a man – a new man.

204

Epilogue

Having hormonally, psychologically, physically and socially transitioned from female to male, I have now lived as a man and been treated as such for over fifteen years. I feel infinitely more at home and comfortable. There are advantages and disadvantages to being male, but this is me.

Some trans people say they feel privileged that they are trans; that this has given them insight into many of the stupidities of gender stereotypes. Although I agree, I would have given anything to have been born a boy, had an adolescence as a boy, and grown up into a man's body without the excruciating attempts of trying to be happy as a woman. I wish I had been able to get hormone blockers to prevent female puberty and then later transition properly; it would have been so much easier.

What seemed like an impossible, unreachable childhood dream came true after a lot of effort and took years to accomplish. I am fortunate that I lived in Europe where it was possible. I haven't married but it's now a legal possibility in Britain for me and for everyone whatever a person's gender. I couldn't have children but this is also now becoming a realistic future possibility through stem cell biology for trans people post-surgery and stigma is fading for those who wish to have children without surgery.

One question is, would I still have had the breakdown and episodes of mania if I hadn't had the gender conflict? It's impossible to know, but I can't help but think the body dysphoria and inner conflict between being male and the lesbian feminist politics of the time was a factor for my mental illness as well as my insecure background.

Nowadays, I'm stable, calmer and people find it difficult to believe that I ever suffered mental health problems at all. Sometimes I think

A New Man

back and remember that at one stage, I was so was unwell I was picking up and collecting rubbish from the street. Being given a home and therefore some security made so much difference to me.

I still despise sexism and I'm still a feminist. I firmly believe that your gender should not stop you from doing anything you want; there should be more flexibility. Children should be free to develop without being forced into rigid gender roles and the policed division of boy's toys and girl's toys and should vanish forever.

You can of course be a masculine woman or a feminine man and everything in-between – that doesn't mean you're trans. Being trans is much more instinctual and about having a fundamental disconnect with your body, that's my perspective anyway.

The imbalance in our society needs to be addressed between men and women. I want women to be more powerful. I am also a firm believer in quotas and positive action for women in business and politics.

In the 2015 General Election, I stood to be an MP for the Green Party. During a television interview, which focussed on me being the first trans man to stand for parliament in the UK, I made a point of stating that parliament did not represent the country properly in terms of the number of women, people from ethnic minorities and people from state schools. I said people like Harvey Milk, the first known gay elected politician, were an inspiration to me and that I thought it was important not to hide that I was trans. I believe that political representation and political power is very important.

My mum died on Mother's Day in 2015, just a few hours before I was due to see her. She died from a progressive incurable lung disease with no known cause. It was upsetting for someone to have such zest for life to have to stop. Marta had such a shaky emotional start in life but she got as much out of life as possible and was always active. Her love and confidence in me, I'm sure helped me be myself.

When I went to the hospital for the death certificate, I wanted to state to the registrar that my mum's year of birth was 1936 as her Colombian passports stated (some said April, some said December) but using

British documentation I had to stick to the date of birth of 1939. I am certain the Colombian documents were the correct ones which meant that Marta died aged 78.

Documentation, such as your birth certificates are important but don't need to define you forever. I think Marta would be pleased that I have now obtained dual nationality and now have a Colombian passport. This also means I have her name now too – my Colombian name is Charlie Kiss Lombard, as Spanish last names include your mother and your father's name.

The Colombian authorities were given my birth certificate, altered to 'boy' since obtaining the Gender Recognition Certificate in 2005 and becoming legally male, so I am listed as M for masculino.

Both my parents saw me transition to male and could tell it was for the best. I am glad about that. Although there was a time when I thought it would be easier to transition if my parents weren't around, it turned out to be far better having their support and in the case of my mum, full support, encouragement and enthusiasm. I was glad of her unending support because, now, I am simply happier.

Note on Terminology

I use the word transsexual in the book, rather than transgender, because it was far more prevalent around the time I transitioned in 2002. In many ways, I feel the term 'transsexual' describes my body dysphoria more accurately. The term transgender is a more recent term- an umbrella term that covers a huge spectrum of different identities and includes non-binary people, (people who don't feel male or female or people who consider that there are many genders) as well as trans men and trans women. The abbreviation 'Trans' cuts through the distinction between transsexual and transgender and so can be a useful word to use.

I am a man and a trans man. I'm both.

I don't mind if people use the word transgender to describe me. It is the 'current' term. I think 'correct' terminology is constantly changing and it's hard for people to keep up with it. The only word I object to is 'tranny'. Even then, when it was used by a friend in a friendly way, I didn't object because the intention was clearly not meant to be offensive, as opposed to the time I was phoned by an anonymous person and called 'a fucking tranny'. So, I would just say to those who are unsure, just ask the person what their preferred term is if using a term about them.

Acknowledgements

There are many people I'd like to thank.

Rebekah deserves thanks for being a loyal and supportive friend. Paul Mattsson helped me through some dark days and I'd like to thank him and friends who stuck by me, such as Kristin, who I'd known since school in York, but who is sadly no longer with us. Thanks to David Musgrove for the encouragement to transition and to Jay Stewart for being a great fellow companion on the transition journey. I'm grateful to Trevor, the first trans man my mum met, and Dru Marland for encouraging me to start writing. I owe a lot to the many trans activists who've got our message out there and who fight for equal rights. I especially want to thank my mother, Marta Lombard, who read the very first draft shortly before she died and was keen for me to write my story.

I'm grateful to all the professional people who helped me to transition- the gender psychiatrists, Dr Russell Reid, and Dr Stuart Lorimer, the surgeons, Dr Dai Davies, Professor Monstrey and Dr Piet Hoebeke, the staff in the hospitals in Belgium and England, the NHS commissioner who enabled me to go to Belgium and last but not least to the many doctors, (in particular, Dr Patfield) and nurses who had to deal with my episodes of mania.

For assisting me with the production of the book, I'd like to acknowledge the following: Dionne McCulloch for copy editing, Robin Yu, for copy editing and proof reading; Jim Jepps for other assistance with writing. Thanks to Leo Kiss for photography and to Laura Salisbury for the book design and typesetting, and to all the helpful people at Troubador Publishing.